$19.95

MODEL RAILWAY KIT BUILDING

W9-CHS-705

MODEL RAILWAY KIT BUILDING

T. J. Booth

PATRICK STEPHENS LIMITED

First published in 1989

British Library Cataloguing in Publication Data
Booth, T.J. (Trevor J)
Model railway kit building.
1. Model railways. Construction
I. Title
625.1'9

ISBN 1–85260–032–2

Patrick Stephens Limited is part of the
Thorsons Publishing Group, Wellingborough,
Northamptonshire NN8 2RQ, England

Typeset by Burns & Smith, Derby
Printed by Biddles Limited, Guildford, Surrey

10 9 8 7 6 5 4 3 2 1

Contents

Introduction

One of the characteristics of the model railway hobby, which sets it apart from many others and contributes significantly to its ability to sustain interest, is the wide variety of tasks involved in producing the model layout. Its production encompasses many aspects, from the basic carpentry of baseboard construction to, ultimately, the running of the completed railway.

There are many diversions involved along the way, and interests can develop in a particular area, such as scenic work or the construction of locomotives and rolling-stock. One thing is sure, if your hobby is model railways it won't be long before you encounter a construction kit of one kind or another, if only a simple plastic kit for a lineside structure, or you may wish to add an item of rolling-stock or a locomotive to your system which is only available in kit form.

The purpose of this book is to help would-be kit-builders to get the best results from the kits they might use for their layouts, and hopefully to encourage those who wish to tackle a more complex kit for, say, a carriage or locomotive, but feel such a construction is beyond them.

It is probably in this latter area of locomotive and rolling-stock construction that the greatest difficulty is experienced, as, inevitably as a result of their very nature, these kits are more complex and not only need to be well finished but must also perform their intended duties on the track to be of any worth. If a further discouragement were needed, then these kits are now quite expensive. All in all, it is perhaps understandable that many are put off what is a very rewarding aspect of the model railway hobby, and indeed can almost become a hobby in itself.

The book was prompted by the comment of a number of retailers, over the years to the effect that, whilst they sell many kits, they doubt that many are ever completed. It is also prompted by the many questions asked of the author at model railway exhibitions about various features and stock on layouts.

It has been my experience that patience and care are more important than any particular skills or an extensive workshop in producing satisfactory models from kits. Indeed, some of the finest models I have seen have been produced in comparatively primitive circumstances.

Hopefully, the book will act as a guide and provide hints and tips on the construction of the various types of kit available, ranging from simple scenic items to complex etched brass locomotive kits. It is intended to smooth the path to the completion of a satisfactory model, provide encouragement and support by showing the methods which I have found have helped me to this end. You will, as your experience and confidence grow, inevitably develop your own approach and methods to the problems you will encounter.

The vast array of kits aimed at the railway modeller, in materials from plastic to brass, and without even considering kits aimed at other hobbies which the railway modeller can call on, makes it impossible to cover all the nuances of kit design or materials, let alone prototype peculiarities. I have therefore chosen to split the subject into three sections; the first, covering locomotives, is, not surprisingly, longer and more detailed.

I have tried to cover the main types of kit available in each section and, whilst not describing in detail the construction of specific kits, I have used, by way of example and for amplification of the text, photographs of a variety of kits under construction. The illustrations predominantly show items under construction, warts and all, rather than the finished product, as these are felt to be more useful and encouraging. I have also avoided comments and assessments of specific kits, as inevitably such views would be personal, and largely subjective.

The model railway press often publishes detailed reviews of kits, and from time to time articles on the construction of specific examples are published. At the end of the day, though, it's up to you. Remember, we all make mistakes and inevitably the models we make will improve with our experience.

I hope the book will demonstrate that anyone can achieve good results from kit building, and will encourage the completion of a few more kits. As with most things in life, there is more than one way of skinning the proverbial cat and so with kit building there are often several alternative ways of achieving the desired result. The methods suggested are ones which have served me well and require the minimum of equipment and technical knowledge, and are thus suited to that well-known beast, the 'kitchen table modeller'.

Acknowledgements

My thanks are due to Bill Morton for his invaluable help with the photographs, and to my wife Susan for typing the manuscript.

SECTION I
Locomotive Construction

For most railway modellers, it is the locomotives that are the principal source of interest, and whilst the modeller in 2mm and particularly 4mm scales is provided with an ever-increasing variety of good quality, ready-to-run items, the locomotives we may want for our layout or collection might not be available. In 7mm scale, you do not now have the luxury of a ready-to-run range at all.

There is a vast range of kits available for steam and diesel locomotives, DMUs and EMUs, principally for 4mm scale, and even some of North American, European and South African proto-

Kit building locomotives enables the modeller to choose from a vast range of locomotives which it is highly unlikely would never be produced as ready-to-run items.

Sadly, plastic has rarely been used for working locomotive kits in Great Britain, one notable exception being the Ratio kit shown.

types in 3.5mm scale. In O gauge there are exciting new ranges of 'state-of-the-art' models appearing from Slaters, Vulcan and Springside.

In recent years, there has been a tremendous improvement in the quality of the kits available generally, and, for the more discerning, some kits can provide, with care, almost museum quality models. They come in a bewildering variety of complexities, materials and designs. It is not possible, therefore, to cover all the types of kit one may meet. However, I have tried to cover in the ensuing pages the common types, materials and assembly methods, and have tried to concentrate on those aspects which are most likely to cause concern.

Do not expect with any model locomotive kit to simply 'shake the box', as it were, and get a finished model. They all require some work by the builder. This should not be allowed to put you off, though, for care and patience are more important than skill in the workshop. Assembly of model locomotive kits will, however, develop skills which can be transferred for use in other aspects of the hobby.

If you are learning to drive, you do not normally start off in a Ferrari, and so it is with building model locomotive kits. Start with something which is straightforward, rather than say a 'Pacific' with outside valve gear, for example. The traditional recommendation is to start with a simple white metal body kit designed to fit on a proprietary ready-to-run chassis, and this has hitherto been sound advice. I would, however, suggest going a stage further and consider beginning with a good quality kit of a simple prototype which requires the building of a chassis from the components supplied.

Before we look at construction itself, a brief outline of the type of kit available and some comment on the tools required, will be worthwhile.

There are basically three types of kit available in the three smaller scales: white metal, etched brass and pre-cut and punched sheet metal. The latter is the oldest of the three, now most common in O gauge, and the traditional method of scratch-building. White metal forms the basis of virtually all N gauge kits which are invariably designed to fit a proprietary chassis, with or without some modification.

In 4mm and 7mm scales, there is an increasing tendency to use a combination of both white metal castings and etchings. This has a number of advantages in that the most appropriate material for a part can be chosen and the two materials bonded together with modern glue or solder. For example, whereas a white metal casting of a cab side sheet will inevitably be too thick, an etched one can give that fineness and thinness of edge so charactertistic of the real thing. How many 6 in thick plate steel cab sides have you seen?

So far as locomotive chassis are concerned, these can be categorized into three main types: cast metal chassis blocks, now mostly associated with the Wills and GEM 4mm scale kits, etched brass, and milled brass, usually now correctly profiled with full detail. The latter two are the only types used in O gauge kits. Chassis kits are, alas, not available for N gauge.

White metal and white metal/etched combinations can be glued together. Whilst I have heard of etched kits being glued, soldering is normally the means of assembly, while the sheet metal kits will certainly require soldered construction. The milled brass chassis are usually screwed together for assembly, whereas the etched type could be designed either for bolt-together assembly, soldered assembly, or may be folded from an etching into a channel section. The techniques of soldering will be discussed later in this section.

CHAPTER 1
Tools and equipment

The list of tools required for locomotive construction is longer than for other areas, but many of those listed are not essential. Those which are considered essential are marked with an asterisk.

A well-equipped workshop is not necessary to assemble loco kits. In the scales we are considering, literally the kitchen table will suffice. Remember, however, that your tool kit will gradually grow as your interest develops after the essential tools are acquired. Bear in mind also that cheap tools are false economy — always buy the best you can afford, because not only will good tools last longer, but they will give you better results and certainly cause less frustration in their use.

Having mentioned the kitchen table, a word of caution. If domestic harmony is to be maintained, it is a good idea to have a piece of blockboard or similar as your work surface to prevent damage to the table or kitchen work surface. This could, if felt necessary, be clamped down, remembering of course to protect the surfaces from the clamp jaws with a piece of felt or similar. This could also be developed into a complete portable workshop, housing tools, bits and pieces and its own power supply. There have been a few detailed articles in the model press over recent years on constructing this type of facility. A simplified sketch giving the overall idea is shown in Figure 1.

Do not forget to look after your tools and equipment; they are not cheap and should be regarded as an asset and an investment. Keep them clean and keep them sharp; it is less likely that accidents will occur using sharp cutting tools than trying to force blunt ones. Replacement knife and saw blades are cheap enough. My suggested list of tools comprises the following:

Swiss or needle files Usually available in sets of five or six, but can be bought individually. I find the flat, round and half round varieties most useful. If used on white metal castings or for removing excess solder, they quickly become clogged, but cleaning with a wire brush will sort this out. Because good quality needle files are quite expensive, I usually keep old worn ones or even buy cheap ones specifically for use on white metal or for cleaning solder.

Pliers Small, long-nosed pliers are essential for bending hand-rails etc, and a general-purpose or engineers' pair is useful.

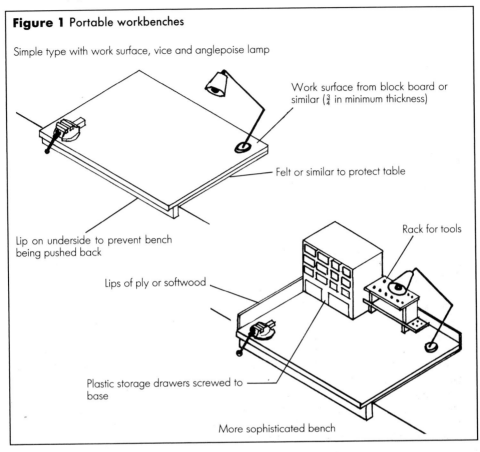

Figure 1 Portable workbenches

Simple type with work surface, vice and anglepoise lamp

Work surface from block board or similar ($\frac{3}{4}$ in minimum thickness)

Felt or similar to protect table

Rack for tools

Lip on underside to prevent bench being pushed back

Lips of ply or softwood

Plastic storage drawers screwed to base

More sophisticated bench

Drills A supply of small twist drills will be essential. Usually, hand-rail knobs and grab-rails need to be drilled with no 68, and no 55 is the tapping size for IO BA screws and bolts, no 50 the clearance size. Other sizes can be bought as necessary if you do not buy a complete drill set. If you do buy a set, buy the set covering sizes in the 80 to 55 range, available from Expo Drills, which will suffice for most purposes and acquire specific supplementary sizes as you need them. These small drills are comparatively expensive and obviously fragile, so keep them clean and sharp and don't force them, particularly if drilling cast metal, as they can easily become stuck and 'lost' in the castings.

Pin chuck A small chuck, sometimes with alternative-sized collets which will hold the very small drills we need to use. It enables a hole to be made by hand by twisting and rotating the chuck between the fingers and thumb. A pin chuck can also be used in a hand drill or even a power drill, but will require great care to ensure that the drill is kept square and no pressure is exerted.

Mini-drill There are a number on the market and they are so versatile a tool that I list them as essential. If you have a mini-drill, a pin chuck is not essential. It will operate from your controller on 12V DC or from its own transformer, and can be used for drilling, sawing, cutting, grinding, polishing, etc; some systems even have their own vertical drill stands, milling attachments and the like.

Screwdrivers A set of jeweller's screwdrivers, sold in plastic wallets containing 4 or 5 different ones, will suffice. One or two 'Phillips' type would be a useful addition.

Soldering-iron For soldering white metal, a low wattage or a temperature-controlled iron is essential, while for etched kits and certainly sheet metal, a substantial wattage iron is needed; there is however, an extensive range on the market. I have a 25 watt iron which I use for white metal and finer etched and sheet parts, and a now rather old 80 watt iron which I have found to be the master of anything I've needed to solder in 7mm scale.

Burnishing tool Essential to clean and polish white metal and brass/nickel parts prior to painting. The pencil type with refills is most suitable.

Vice I hesitate to suggest a vice as essential, but it is one of those tools which, once you have one, you never know how you managed before. It is handy for holding white metal whilst it is filed and cut, holding sheet or etched metal parts whilst they are being bent and, of course, for holding parts whilst being soldered. A vice with jaws open-ing to 3 or 4 in will suffice for even O gauge. It is essential to ensure that the jaws close accurately together.

Try-square A small engineers' square is very useful for checking the square-ness of components and assemblies such as cabs or tank sides.

Razor-saw For fine cuts in thin metal and plastic, the type with inter-changeable or replacement blades such as the 'X Acto' is best.

Taps Taper taps of 8 and 10 BA for 4mm scale and 6 and 8 BA in 7mm scale enable threads to be tapped into parts to enable fixing by bolts. Often a nut can be soldered over a pre-drilled clea-rance hole to avoid using a tap.

G-clamps Minature G-clamps are avail-able in sets of three and may be useful to hold certain parts together.

Junior hacksaw For cutting heavier metals such as frame brass, etc.

Calipers/dividers Useful in scratch-building and in extensive kit modifica-tion to transfer dimensions from a drawing.

Wet-and-dry papers Use medium to fine grades for finishing parts before assembly and in the final preparation before painting.

There will be other tools and pieces of equipment which you will find useful as your expertise develops and you find your own methods. For example, I keep broken and blunted craft knife blades for scraping solder and paring down white metal. Old toothbrushes are useful for cleaning up models prior to painting, and I find hair-grips useful for holding small parts together whilst soldering. Blu-Tack is similarly useful.

CHAPTER 2
Soldering and 'superglue'

Sooner or later the need to solder will arise. There have been several learned treatises in the model press on the technicalities of soft soldering. This chapter is intended as a brief practical guide to the essentials. If you have any doubts, practise on some scrap metal, cut up a tin can or whatever, but do have a go. It is not nearly as difficult as it seems.

As with most aspects of model building, there are a few basic principles. The first is common to many other aspects, and this is cleanliness. The metal to be joined must be clean and grease free where the solder is to run, so clean the parts in this area with wet-and-dry or the burnishing tool. The second is the right solder for the job. Basically, multicore solder is sufficient for sheet and etched metal kits and low-melt solder for white metal kits, but there are now a number of solders on the market, such as the Carr's range, which offer a variety of melting point temperatures. These offer certain advantages where a number of parts are built up to form detail; it is useful when fixing the last part not to have need of so much heat that the other parts in the assembly become unsoldered!

The third essential is to have sufficient heat for the job in hand. It is no good trying to solder an O gauge chassis of $\frac{1}{16}$ th in brass to brass frame spacers with a 25 watt iron. Conversely, apply too much heat to white metal and instead of a set of nicely-detailed cast parts, you will have a pool of molten alloy!

A flux is needed to wipe the intended joint where the solder will flow. A phosphoric acid flux such as Eames 40 Flux is ideal. Avoid the use of Bakers Fluid, as this is very corrosive.

Practise a simple 90° joint on sheet or etched metal. Check that the two parts are a good, accurate fit, square and true, and make a simple wooden jig to hold them whilst the hot iron is applied. Clean the edges of the individual pieces to be soldered and wipe them with flux with a small brush. Hold the iron on the edge of each piece where the flux has been applied, then bring the solder to the iron where it touches the metal and, moving the iron along the edge, coat with a thin, even film of solder, and smooth out any blobs. This process is known as tinning, next, place the parts against the wooden jig as they are to be assembled, hold the iron on the joint, and slide it steadily along its length. The solder from the previously tinned edges should flow together and, when the iron is removed and the metal allowed to cool for a few seconds, the joint should be made. It's as simple as that. It is quite possible to add more solder and flux to improve the joint should this be necessary.

It is not always possible to tin the components before assembly and, in this case, the parts should be held together, the joint wiped with flux and the iron applied. The solder is then introduced to the iron, which is wiped down the joint.

On small joints at short edges etc, it will be sufficient to add the solder to the heated joint surfaces. In many instances, it will be sufficient to merely touch a joint for a few seconds.

The most common failure of soldered joints is what is known as a 'dry joint'. This is invariably caused because the joint has not been heated enough for the solder to flow correctly. It is easy to tell if the solder is flowing correctly, and therefore hot enough, because it will become a bright shiny silver. As it cools, it becomes more grey in colour.

Solder assembly of white metal kits is a different kettle of fish. Because the melting point of the cast metal is so low, great care needs to be taken to avoid melting the components along with the solder. The melting point of ordinary solder is higher than that of the casting, therefore special low-melting-point solder is called for, together with a low-wattage iron.

The basic soldering procedure outlined above is followed, though I find rather than tinning the parts it is easier to introduce the low-melt solder to the fluxed joint along with the iron. The trick is to allow the iron to be there just long enough for the solder to flow. You have to move away with the soldering iron very rapidly to avoid melting adjacent parts, especially if working in a confined area such as the inside of a tank or cab. For safety's sake, I confine soldering white metal kits to the main structural components, using 'superglue' for finer parts and details.

I find it easier and safer to use my 25 watt iron quickly, rather than a smaller iron for longer, on the basis that the hotter iron, moved quickly, gives less heat build-up than the smaller iron used for longer periods at the same place. I do not know whether there is any scientific support for this theory — it's just my preference.

There will be occasions when it is necessary to solder white metal parts to sheet metal. Here, the procedure is to tin the sheet metal with low-melt solder, apply flux to this area, hold the cast component in place and, by holding the iron on the sheet metal adjacent to, but not near enough to melt, the casting, 'sweat' the casting on (ie hold it into the molten tinning). Remove the iron and allow the joint to cool.

'Superglue' is marvellous stuff, providing it is used properly. It can, like most of the materials and substances used in modelling, be dangerous if misused. The essential criteria which must be met if the joint to be made is to be strong and successful are as follows:

1 The joint must be closely and accurately made and held still until the glue sets — only a few seconds.

2 The surfaces to be joined must be spotlessly clean and above all free from grease. Run the burnishing tool over

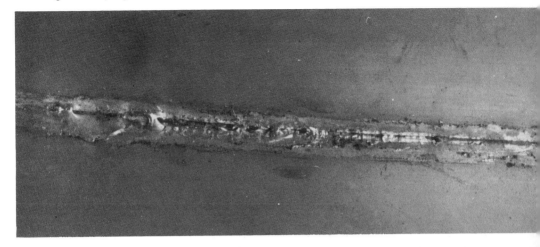

Above *An example of a bad solder joint as described in the text. The solder has not flowed at all and a very insecure joint is the result. The probable reasons were insufficient heat, the iron being moved along too quickly and the components not held together well enough whilst soldering — a gap is apparent at the centre.*

Right *A well-soldered joint.*

the edges to be bonded and do not put your fingers over them before gluing the parts.

3 Use the glue sparingly. The more glue that is used, the greater the setting time and the weaker the joint. Place a small amount, a pin-head-sized dot, on a piece of non-porous material and dip a pin or similar into this to apply the glue to the areas to be stuck.

CHAPTER 3
Construction preliminaries

Preparation is all important before the construction of a locomotive kit begins, not just in the obvious sense of ensuring you have all the parts to complete the model to hand and the necessary glues and solders, but also in the choice of prototype for your model.

It is essential to pick a particular locomotive of a class suitable for the period you are modelling if you are to produce an accurate model. If you think that is taking things a bit too far, then consider the situation of so-called standard classes such as the LMS Class '5' or '5XP' 'Jubilee'. The former had several different configurations of boiler fittings; the original batch had domeless boilers and cross-head pumps which were removed in the late 1930s, while some had rivetted tenders of the 4,000 gallon type, some all-welded, and they carried various valve gears, not to mention detail differences and livery changes. The '5XP' 'Jubilees' had three different boilers, two different fireboxes (which do change the visual appearance slightly), four different tender possibilities, and two unique rebuilt members of the class, to name but a few differences. Even more humble locomotives, such as the

Brighton 'Terriers', had a bewildering variety of appearances, so do not think that the older, smaller classes escape.

There are two sources of information: drawings and photographs. Unless you are making major alterations to dimensions or appearance, photographs are to be preferred as they provide an accurate and detailed record of the appearance of a locomotive at the time the picture was taken. Drawings may only be of one unspecified class member at a particular time, and not all published drawings are 100 per cent accurate in detail. Do not, however, trust photographs of preserved locomotives, as compromises may have been necessary in restoration, and in all probability the locomotive will be preserved in its final condition, irrespective of the period of the livery it sports.

There are plenty of photographs of locomotives, even at the turn of the century, which in all probability will provide the necessary information, and thankfully these are largely available in the many published photographic and detailed locomotive books, some of which are listed in Appendix I. If by any chance you cannot find the picture you need from the many books available, prints from large and comprehensive historical photograph collections are usually available at a small charge. Try Real Photographs, Terminal House, Shepperton, Middlesex TW 17 8AS; Lens of Sutton, 4 Westmead Road, Sutton, Surrey; or Wild Swan Photographic Dept, 12 Western Road, Henley on Thames, Oxon. There are other collections also available and advertised in the model press from time to time.

Having decided on the model you are to build and purchased the necessary kit, some preparation is required before the parts are assembled. The first step is to check the parts against the list of components shown on the instruction sheet. This is not as silly as it sounds, because kits often contain sets of parts in plastic bags, others wrapped in tissue, and sometimes have delicate parts taped to the inside of the box lid.

This also helps in identifying the parts and can save much heartache later if a part is missing or, perhaps, where a similar part has been used incorrectly by mistake.

The next step is to study the instruction sheet carefully, to familiarize yourself with the order of assembly. Usually an exploded diagram is included which is helpful, and it is particularly important to identify the order of assembly, as some parts can only be fitted at a certain stage of construction. It is also quite easy to fix parts upside down or slightly in the wrong place. It's easily done, as I know to my cost! When you have identified the parts and the assembly sequence, have a dry run, holding the parts in place with Blu-Tack, hair-grips, rubber bands etc on white metal kits to get the feel of the model and check the fit of the parts — of which more later.

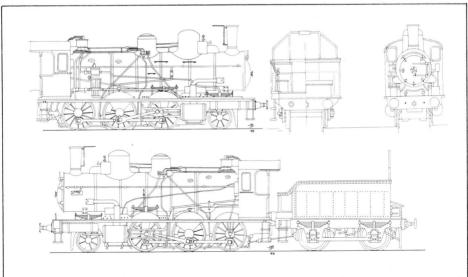

A typical scale drawing used in building a model locomotive, in this case a SNCF 130B.
Scale 2mm = 1ft

CHAPTER 4
The chassis

Building

It is impossible to suggest a firm order of assembly which will cover all kits because the individual designs of both the kit and prototype will require a different sequence. It is of paramount importance to assemble the chassis first (or have the chassis available if a ready-to-run example is being used with a body-only kit) in order that the locomotive body can be built over the chassis and all necessary clearances for wheels and valve gear ensured. It is much easier to remove a bit of body material before it is assembled than to try and scrape a few thou from inside some dark nook or cranny of an assembled body. Indeed, it is not always easy to identify exactly where fouling occurs. By building or acquiring the chassis first, it is a straightforward matter to check the fit and clearances of the footplate assembly and to continue to check as parts are added.

Do not assume that because a chassis is included with a kit or sold specifically to go with a body that it will automatically be a perfect fit. Manufacturing processes alone may account for some minor discrepancy, but design faults do occur. I have had complete kits where the wheel spacings for splashers on the running-plate did not match those of the chassis, rendering the marrying of the two impossible without major alteration. Had I assembled the body first, I would have had great difficulty doing anything about it. Thankfully, major problems of this kind are becoming the exception. If you do have problems, such as missing or damaged parts or a breakage during assembly, do not hesitate to contact the manufacturers, who are usually most helpful. Indeed, if you do not tell them of the problems you encounter, how can they rectify them in later batches or improve them?

In many respects the chassis is the most important part of the locomotive because, however nice your finished model looks, if the chassis is not right then it will not work. If it will not work, then you are going to be disillusioned and none to keen to have a go at another kit, thus missing out on a very rewarding aspect of the hobby.

Again, individual chassis designs and kits have variations, but the general principles outlined in the ensuing paragraphs should be a helpful guide.

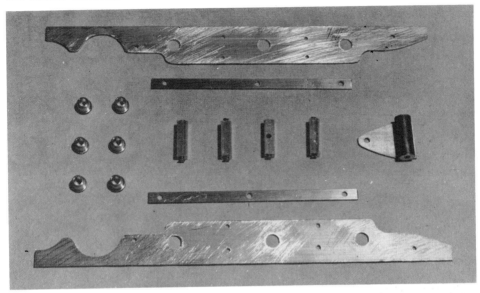

A basic brass chassis for bolt-together assembly. Brass 'top hat' bearings are provided but the coupling rods, whilst drilled, require filing to shape and detailing. This type of chassis kit requires a fair amount of work by the builder and should not be confused with the high quality, detailed and consequently more expensive kits on the market.

Figure 2 Checking accuracy of chassis

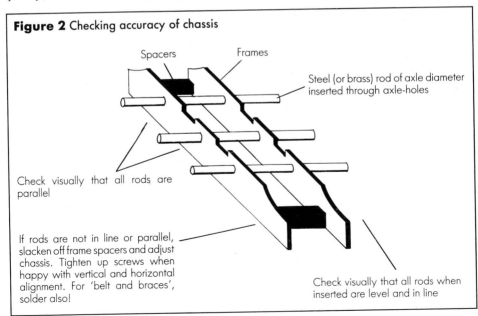

Spacers

Frames

Steel (or brass) rod of axle diameter inserted through axle-holes

Check visually that all rods are parallel

If rods are not in line or parallel, slacken off frame spacers and adjust chassis. Tighten up screws when happy with vertical and horizontal alignment. For 'belt and braces', solder also!

Check visually that all rods when inserted are level and in line

Remember that the manufacturer's instructions should be read and followed to the letter, particularly in regard to sequences of assembly and methods.

The prime requirement for any chassis is that it is square and true. Assembly on a flat, true surface, such as a piece of plate glass, is helpful. There are, however, a number of ways in which the squareness of the chassis can be checked, such as that shown in Figure 2.

The solid cast or milled chassis block is usually by its very nature square. Any adjustment with these chassis blocks is usually to ensure that they locate under the footplate correctly and that any retaining lugs fit their respective sockets. This is easily checked against the body parts, and any changes found necessary can be achieved with judicious filing. Remember to take it easy — you can always take off a little bit more, but you can't put it back! Also

Left *The standard OO gauge wheel from Romford, rather coarse when compared with the Maygib shown in the next picture.*

Below *A Maygib driving wheel set showing the shouldered axle, finer tread and accurate spokes.*

Below right *The finer wheels in use on an 0–4–4 chassis. The Hamblings-type crankpins have been used and do not look too bad.*

remember to ensure that the footplate is kept flat whilst checking the chassis fit. It is quite easy for the footplate to be slightly bent or twisted before the body is built up on it, and that can accommodate the odd millimetre which may make all the difference.

Cast or milled chassis are probably the easiest to assemble, particularly if the recommended motor is used. By their very nature it can be difficult to modify them to take motors requiring different methods of mounting.

On the subject of motors, much detailed technical appraisal has been given in the model railway press in recent years on the performance and efficiency of different motors, and of motors with different combinations of gear ratios and wheel sizes. Suffice to say for the purposes of a general look at the subject that the current crop of motors, such as Anchoridge, Mashima, Sagami, etc, give very satisfactory results. Then, at a price there is the Kean

Maygib Portescap range of coreless motors and gear boxes, which are really the 'Rolls-Royce' variety. They are expensive, and may require modification of your control system to get the best results. They require very little power, are very efficient mechanically and give a very smooth performance and control, but only, of course, in an accurately assembled chassis.

There is a wide selection of wheels available to the 4mm scale modeller, the most common of which is the Romford range. These are easy to use and, with one exception, are general-purpose wheels sold by their diameter, eg 20mm, 26mm, etc. They are available in insulated or uninsulated form, so that current collectors will be needed either on one side only or on both sides if all insulated wheels are used. For the more discerning, there are finer wheels which are actually modelled on prototype wheels and are sold by size, crank-pin position and

prototype application. Such wheels are not suitable for use on coarse track-work, but are worth considering, however, if you have a modern finescale track system, as they improve appearance no end, as can be seen from the illustration. Sources for this type of wheel are the Alan Gibson or Maygib ranges, or from the most extensive range of all produced by Mike Sharman and available by mail order.

In 7mm scale, there are traditional cast-iron driving wheels which are available turned and finished for two-rail finescale operation with insulation either at the rim or through the spokes. These are readily available for most common sizes from 'Home of O Gauge', Wednesbury Wheels and CCW. Alternatively, Slaters and Alan Gibson produce a growing range of slightly cheaper, very accurate wheels in nylon with steel tyres. Each range has a crank-pin system designed and marketed for use with it. Similarly, bogie and tender wheels are also available in all these types.

Poor current collection is, in my experience, the most common cause of running problems. There are various favoured systems for current collection but the two basic methods are the plunger pick-up system and variations on the age-old wheel wiper. There is a school of thought which tends to denigrate the wiper system in favour of plunger pick-ups. I have used both systems in 4mm scale and in O gauge. Both work and both have advantages and disadvantages; the key to the plunger system is to keep the plunger free from grease and gunge, which may restrict its freedom to move out with the wheel and, in soldering the wire link from the motor, to ensure that this does not restrict the movement either because the wire is too near the plunger housing or because the wire used is too thick.

A traditional type of chassis showing wiper-type pick-ups operating from an insulated block on to the rear of the wheel tyres.

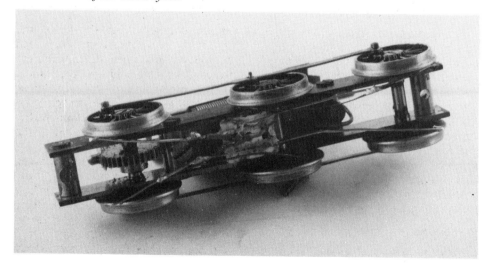

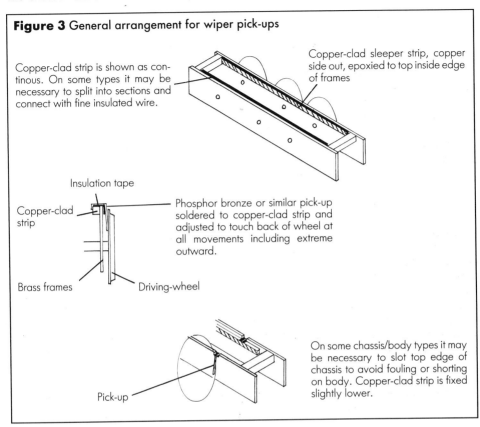

Figure 3 General arrangement for wiper pick-ups

Copper-clad strip is shown as continous. On some types it may be necessary to split into sections and connect with fine insulated wire.

Copper-clad sleeper strip, copper side out, epoxied to top inside edge of frames

Insulation tape

Copper-clad strip

Phosphor bronze or similar pick-up soldered to copper-clad strip and adjusted to touch back of wheel at all movements including extreme outward.

Brass frames

Driving-wheel

On some chassis/body types it may be necessary to slot top edge of chassis to avoid fouling or shorting on body. Copper-clad strip is fixed slightly lower.

Pick-up

The wiper system must have wipers which are carefully adjusted not to exert too much pressure or springing on the backs of wheels, but to have sufficient pressure to keep contact. The system shown in Figure 3 has become my favoured system. It requires little adjustment and maintenance, is neat and unobtrusive and applicable to most types of chassis. I would not use anything else in 4mm scale, but I find the plungers, particularly the large Vulcan type, very satisfactory in O gauge.

Assembly

Having studied the instructions, familiarized yourself with the parts and intended assembly sequence, and acquired the parts needed to finish the model, such as the glues, solders and tools, we can begin with the actual construction. The following paragraphs apply to 4mm or 7mm scales, and specific attention is drawn to the characteristics of each scale.

Assembly will begin with the chassis, either assembling the frames or finishing the castings. For the purpose of this exercise, a traditional rigid chassis is assumed — more of compensation later. Milled brass chassis blocks will probably require little attention as they are usually supplied finished. White metal chassis blocks will, however, probably require the attention of a file to clean off any flash or moulding lines.

Check that the holes in the chassis block for the body/chassis locating screws have enough clearance and adjust if necessary by either drilling with the correct clearance size, 50 for 10 BA, or 43 for 8 BA, or rotating a small round needle file in the hole. Similarly, check the clearances for any other screw holes.

The chassis will either be pre-drilled to take $\frac{1}{8}$ in diameter standard 4mm scale axles, the usual practice with milled brass, or to take $\frac{1}{8}$ in inside diameter brass 'top hat' bearings. In O gauge, these are $\frac{5}{16}$ in outside diameter for $\frac{3}{16}$ in driving wheel axles. These bearings are a push fit into the chassis block and are there to protect the chassis; it is easier to replace a worn bearing than build a new chassis. In practice, a considerable amount of usage over many years will be necessary before any noticeable signs of bearing wear occur, so do not worry about this. Check that the axles rotate freely in their holes. It may be necessary to run the round file through either axle hole or top hat bearing to ensure the essential free movement. Do not overdo it, however, for if the axles slip about, particularly in a horizontal, front to back plane, a poor-running chassis will ensue, if indeed it runs at all. Some vertical movement can occur to advantage, how-

Etched brass chassis kits provide considerable detail, down to the bolt-heads and rivets. They may be designed to be assembled on to spacers or, as in the case of the one shown here, folded from flat into a channel.

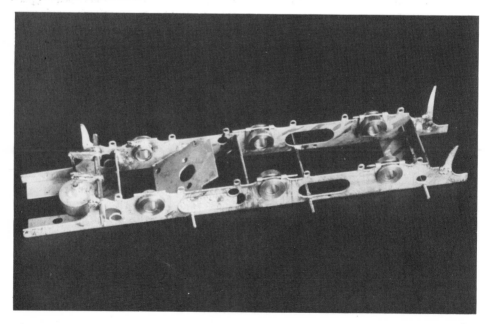

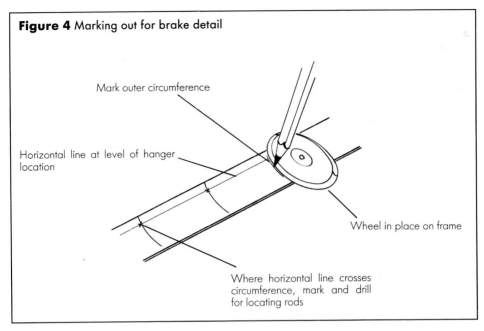

Figure 4 Marking out for brake detail

Mark outer circumference

Horizontal line at level of hanger location

Wheel in place on frame

Where horizontal line crosses circumference, mark and drill for locating rods

ever, and if possible I tend to allow a slight vertical movement, particularly on the centre axle.

Once the axles rotate freely, consideration can be given to adding brake detail, or more precisely making the necessary preparations. The next few lines relate to those chassis which make no provision for brake detail, but its provision is, I feel, even in 4mm scale, essential to the appearance of the finished model.

Place one wheel on an axle and place this in each axle hole (with the bearing in place if one is fitted) and mark with a pencil the circumference of the wheel on the chassis. Check by reference to photographs or drawings the locations of the brake hangers in relation to the wheel, specifically their height, and by comparing this to the cast or moulded brake hangers to be used on the model, find the height on the chassis from

which they will hang. Usually this is required once only on each side. Again with a pencil and with the aid of a straight edge, mark a line at this point along the length of the chassis side. Where the line crosses the line around the circumference of the wheel, a hole will need to be drilled to hang the brakes (see Figure 4).

There are a number of brake mouldings and castings available in both 4mm and 7mm and one can usually be found which is suitable for the model. The plastic ones avoid the risk of shorting on the wheels, but a more restricted range is available. On cast and solid brass chassis, it is sufficient to drill $\frac{1}{8}$ in or so into the chassis and to mount the brake hangers on a track pin with the head reduced in size, or a short length of hand-rail or similar wire fixed into the hole.

Usually, etched chassis, incorporat-

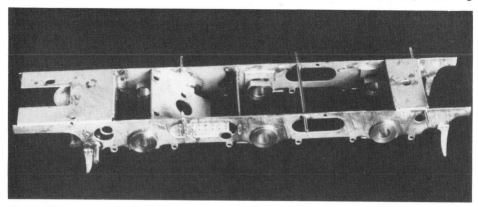

Above *The supports for brake hangers crossing the chassis as described in the text are clearly shown, as is the rear pivot, similarly fitted, for the brake linkage. The flat tops on the centre and forward bearings are to accommodate an equalizing bar which pivots between the two in this type of compensated chassis.*

Below *In addition to the detail, such as the representation of the firebox sides, a feature of etched chassis is often the location of parts by 'slot and tab' such as the motor mounting plate. Modern kits often combine a variety of materials such as the cast metal vacuum cylinder seen here.*

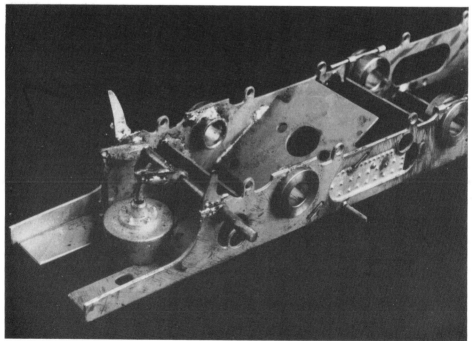

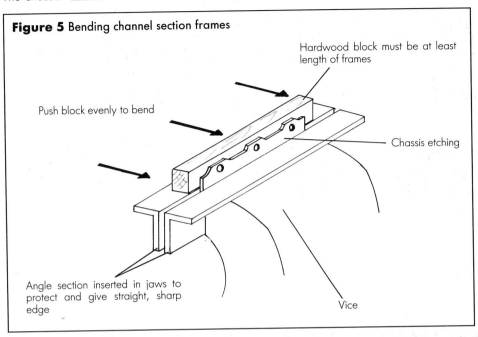

Figure 5 Bending channel section frames

Hardwood block must be at least length of frames

Push block evenly to bend

Chassis etching

Angle section inserted in jaws to protect and give straight, sharp edge

Vice

ing more detail anyway than cast chassis, include provision for brake detail as do those, particularly in O gauge, in which milled brass side-frames, assembled on spacers, form the chassis. However, there are some chassis of this type, predominately in 4mm scale, in which no provision is made for hanging brakes. The same procedure outlined above is followed, except that it is done before the chassis side members are assembled; and the hanger can be a piece of wire or rod-ding which goes through both frames, as shown in the photographs.

Those chassis which require assembly of frames with some form of spacer or stretcher between, require care to ensure that they are square, and can be conveniently assembled on a piece of plate glass. Adjustment to ensure squareness is easy with the bolt-together type, but where soldered stretchers are used, great care is necess-ary. Usually the design is intended to minimize this difficulty, and the kit instructions should be scrutinized care-fully to ensure that this essential point is followed. The frames can be painted at this stage before the wheels etc are assembled, and any details added. Any subsequent damage to the paint surface can be dealt with later.

The fold-up type of chassis is self-aligning, providing care is taken in bending it squarely and accurately. Here it is of assistance to use a vice and steel bars (wooden blocks can be used at a pinch) at least the length of the chassis. This is used to bend the etched chassis over at a sharp angle to form the section required, and the method is shown in Figure 5.

Before the wheels can be mounted in

the chassis, the question of gears needs to be addressed. There are a great many variations of gear boxes, gear cradles and motor mounting systems on the market, particularly for 4mm scale, and to a large extent the choice of transmission system will need to be considered integrally with the motor.

Whatever system is used, the gear will need to be mounted on the axle securely before the wheels, coupling rods and, where applicable, valve gear, are assembled. The usual method of securing the gear on the axle is by a grub-screw, but it is not good practice to rely on the grub-screw alone on the round surface of the axle. I have found that the simple expedient of filing a flat on the axle which will locate the gear works well and provides the grub-screw with a good grip.

The worm which fits on to the motor shaft in a conventional worm and gear drive may similarly have a collar and be fixed with a grub-screw. The final fixing of the worm, if no grub-screw arrangement is provided, can be accomplished quite easily by the use of Loctite or similar.

If you buy your worm and gearwheel separately, be careful to ensure that your worm is bored to the correct size for the motor shaft. A suitable brass sleeve may be sold with the motor or bought from the same source to fit on the shaft to fit exactly the worm bore.

Now the wheels should be fixed in place. The Romford system in 4mm scale, and now virtually all 7mm scale wheels, have square-ended axles which makes it a straightforward job to 'bolt on' the wheels and ensure immediate quartering and correct gauge. Quartering, in simple terms, is ensuring that the crank-pin bosses are on each side parallel and at 90° to those on the opposite side.

The finer 4mm scale wheels already

The chassis, with cast springs, brakes and cylinder covers, has been primed and awaits spraying black and reassembly.

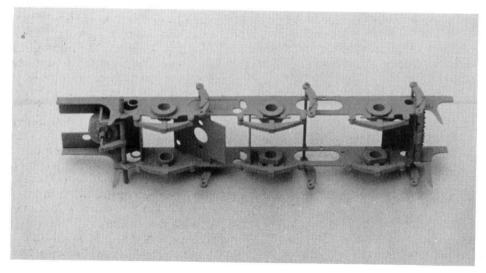

mentioned do not have the convenience of self-quartering. However, quartering is not a difficult job even if these wheels are used, the wheels being pressed home on their axles at the desired position and twisted and tweaked until correctly positioned. One easy way of checking is by looking through the wheels and aligning the spokes with those on the opposite side. The finer wheels are often supplied with alternative axles for OO and EM gauge (specific axles and wheels with finer treads and flanges for 18.83 S4). The axles are either shouldered or tapered, the wheel being pressed home on the axle and being at the correct gauge when the shoulder is reached. Other wheels merely come with a length of $\frac{1}{8}$ in diameter rod for the axles which must be cut to length and the wheels very carefully gauged. It is unlikely that any of these 'push-on' type wheels will be 100 per cent true; the axle must be rotated and the wheel 'tweaked' gently until it runs accurately. There is also the Hamblings wheel press tool available from Eames of Reading which, used in the vice, presses wheels on to axles squarely, and by using ready-fitted crank-pins, sets the wheels at the correct quartering.

Romford wheels, in 4mm scale and O gauge can generally be taken from and reassembled on their axles many times with impunity, which is handy for painting, repairs and detailing. With the push-on types, however, it is not recommended that once installed they be removed from their axles if it is possible to avoid doing so — which it should be with careful planning. Do not worry too much if you have to, though; I have had EM locos where for various reasons

I have needed to remove wheels from their axles more than once, and they have survived. If they do become loose on their axles, a spot of Loctite or similar will hold them securely.

Not only does painting the wheels before assembly save one possible reason for removing them from their axles, but it is also much easier than trying to paint them when mounted on the chassis.

Each wheel range tends to have its own specifically designed crank-pin system to go with it, but these are not always easy to obtain and, though some may regard it as sacrilege, I have used the Romford type in the finer 4mm wheel systems with great success and, in my opinion, no visual detriment. The pre-moulded crank-pin hole is simply drilled out with a No 55 and the brass crank-pin tapped into this. I file the already thin retaining washers as thinly as practical before fixing them in place on the crank-pin. Well cleaned and fluxed, the merest touch of soldering iron will fix the washers to the pin without damaging the plastic-centred wheels. Alternatively, a touch of 'super-glue' applied sparingly on the end of the pin could be used. The crank-pin is cut down afterwards and filed smooth to neaten its appearance. It is useful to place a small piece of thin paper between the coupling rod and the retaining washer which can be pulled away after the latter is soldered to the pin. This prevents the coupling rod and crank pin washer being soldered together and also allows a small degree of lateral movement on the crank pin, which will help with slow running. Crank-pins are supplied in O gauge with Slaters wheels and substantial turned steel ones are available for cast-

Above *An etched chassis completed and ready for painting, showing the features mentioned in the text, particularly the plunger pick-ups.*

Below *The builder may well need to make his own arrangements to mount the motor in some kits. A simple plate, drilled to take the motor fixing screws and soldered between the frames, is shown here.*

Great care is needed in mounting a motor to ensure correct meshing of worm and gear. For the arrangement shown, the plate is mounted on the motor, the motor positioned with the worm on the gear wheel with a cigarette paper between to aid the correct spacing between the worm and gear. When the motor is correctly positioned, the mounting plate is tack soldered in place as shown. The motor is then removed and the soldered joint completed.

iron wheels. These screw into pre-drilled and tapped holes in the wheels, and are shouldered for the coupling rod.

Now, having just assembled the wheels, motor gears and coupling rods, is the time to check the chassis for running, whether you have outside valve gear or not. If it runs well at the first try, you have been lucky — leave it! More than likely there will be some stiffness and binding, so check the wheel quartering. This should be spot-on if self-quartering wheels are used, so it is more likely that the coupling rods

are binding and the cure is simple, even if not in the interest of furthering pure mechanical engineering — open the crank pin holes slightly.

Outside valve gear often causes problems. The approaches in 4mm and 7mm scale are somewhat different in assembly practice even if the general principle is the same.

In 4mm scale, the valve gear will, in all probability, be etched and supplied in an etched fret from which the parts must be removed. Assembly will be by rivet and possibly the odd pin and screw. In 7mm scale, the valve gear

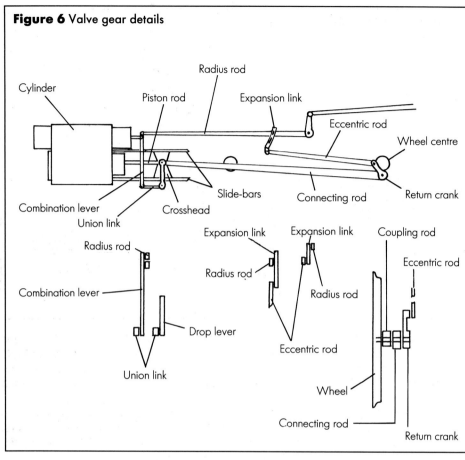

Figure 6 Valve gear details

may similarly be etched or may be milled and nickel-plated. Assembly in this scale can be by nut and bolt, rather than rivets. Valve gear components, and for that matter coupling rods, are usually a good deal thicker than some kit manufacturers think and in O gauge, where etched valve gear is used, it is usual to have to 'sweat' the two pieces together to achieve the desired thickness. The milled type with bolt assembly calls for little constructional comment.

The following notes on etched valve gear assembly are aimed at 4mm scale but, except for the need to substitute nuts and bolts for rivets in assembly and to 'sweat' together parts to build up thickness, the idea is the same. The first stage is to identify the respective parts. Usually the valve gear encountered is Walschaerts and a diagram of this (Figure 6) is provided to identify the parts.

The etched valve gear will require removal from its fret; an old chisel or strong knife blade is recommended rather than tin snips which may distort the parts. Do not forget that the fluting,

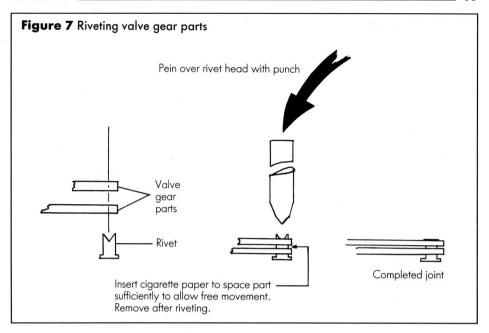

Figure 7 Riveting valve gear parts

Pein over rivet head with punch

Valve gear parts

Rivet

Insert cigarette paper to space part sufficiently to allow free movement. Remove after riveting.

Completed joint

if there is any, will be outermost, and therefore such parts will be handed. It is usual for a detailed assembly order to be provided, but the essential points are shown in Figure 6.

Before assembly begins, clean any burrs from the parts and rub lightly over the front and back near where they have been cut, thus eliminating one possible source of binding. Identify also those holes which require rivets and those which need pins, and ensure that the holes will take the rivets supplied. The fit of the rivets must not be sloppy, neither must it be so tight as to impede movement, as the rivets and pins will act as pivots for the moving valve gear components.

The method of joining valve gear components with rivets is shown in Figure 7. The rivet is placed head down, the valve gear parts placed on it and the hollowed end, which is uppermost,

peined over with light taps of the hammer. A punch is a useful tool to aid this process, the punch being placed on the hollow end of the rivet, and hit with the

Etched valve gear and coupling rods. The latter are sweated together on each side and their design provides a jointed rod essential for compensation.

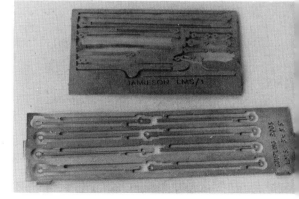

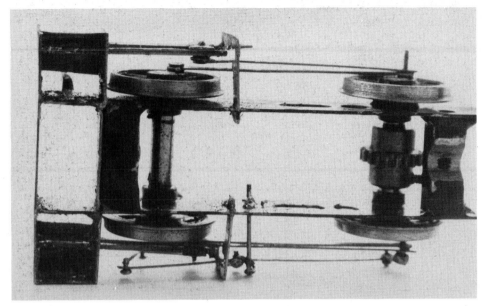

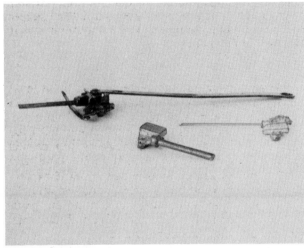

Above _A chassis under construction showing the pin-and-solder method of fixing the valve gear components together._

Left _A selection of cast crossheads and piston rods available from the trade and, at the top, a crosshead assembled with connecting rod. Note the bar added behind to keep the crosshead in line with the slide bars. The crosshead should be free and easy in movement but not sloppy, otherwise it may lock or foul causing, at worst, damage to the rest of the valve gear._

hammer. Do not make the rivet too tight, as it must be free to move — check at each stage of the assembly. The movement, and the correct fit of the rivet, can be more or less guaranteed by placing a piece of thin paper between the valve gear parts being riveted. Cigarette paper is ideal.

The crosshead and piston rod is usually a casting, and contains provision for fixing the union link and combination lever. Usually these parts are riveted together, and then the union link to the crosshead. Be careful when

An example of the very tight clearances between crosshead and connecting rod assembly and the leading crank pin of an outside cylinder locomotive, referred to in the text. The crank pin and securing nut will require filing down to enable the necessary clearance to be assured. The motion bracket holding the slide bars can also be seen.

riveting to a cast crosshead not to snap it. I find that with soft white metal crossheads which contain a cast link to the union link, it is easier, and safer, to fix the union link with a pin inserted through the components from the front and soldering (with low-melt solder) or gluing the pin at the back, finally snipping off and filing down the excess length of pin shaft.

The cylinders are often cast metal, and naturally the specific kit instructions for fixing should be followed. They call for little comment other than again to ensure that the slide bars are parallel and that they are firmly fixed at the correct angle in the cylinders. The crosshead should be a smooth and easy fit, but not sloppy, and slide smoothly between the slide bars. The motion bracket, if one is provided, is a help in this as it holds the slide bars in place. Careful fitting of this before finally fixing will hold the bars at the correct distance and steady. File down any protruding bits at the rear of the crosshead and in particular ensure that the fixing screw or bolt, joining the crosshead to the connecting rod, does not foul the coupling rod.

Etched cylinders usually require the assembly of wrappers around cylinder ends. This is definitely a job for soldering and is straightforward enough providing that the cylinder wrapper is pre-curved to the shape of the ends. Plenty of flux and a hot iron on well-tinned components, with the iron

A selection of cylinders showing (right) the best set made from etched components — tricky but worth the trouble.

moved along the joint at each end, should do the trick, although a little fiddly. If the cylinder ends are etched and require detail to be built up, do this after the cylinder wrapper is soldered on and use a lower temperature solder.

In O gauge it is usual for cylinders to be cast, and these may well be solid blocks of white metal which require drilling for slide bars, piston rod and valve spindle. Beware when drilling into heavy blocks of white metal that the drill does not bind, stick, and break. Remove the drill regularly during drilling and keep the job well lubricated.

The return crank on 4mm scale models usually requires soldering to the crank pin. Neatness is required to allow the return crank rod to pass over the return crank when the gear is in motion. Not much heat is required in 4mm scale, but beware of damaging the plastic-centred wheel or loosening a moulded-in crank-pin.

In O gauge, the return crank is soldered on to the crank-pin, and in this scale the crank may be substantial enough to be partly drilled to accept a shouldered end to the crank-pin. Alternatively, a nut may be soldered on the inner side of the crank where thinner etched valve gear is used, and this is then screwed on to the threaded crank-pin. This can be held permanently in position by a touch of 'superglue'. This method is particularly useful where plastic-centred wheels are used, to avoid the risk of damage from the heat of the soldering iron.

Once the valve gear is assembled and the chassis moves satisfactorily in both directions, with no binding, we can think of current collectors, except where plunger pick-ups have been used, and these will, of necessity, have been fitted earlier. Figure 3 showed the arrangements of wiper collectors and these have been discussed earlier. Ensure that the collectors are functioning properly and touch all the wheel rims at all extreme movements in relation to the chassis. The more wheels that pick up current from the track, the better, and obviously all driving wheels should be so arranged. It is equally effective and usually quite simple to arrange current collection from bogie and tender wheels also, as Figure 8 demonstrates.

Once the collectors are in place and the loco wired up and moving satisfactorily, it is best to run it in. Using a light machine oil, or indeed one specially

Figure 8 Arranging current collection from bogie/pony trucks

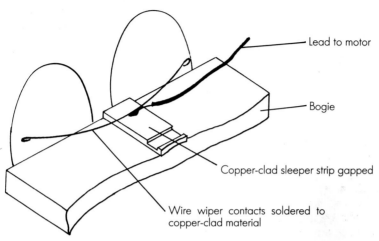

Lead to motor

Bogie

Copper-clad sleeper strip gapped

Wire wiper contacts soldered to copper-clad material

Figure 9 Arrangements for springing bogies to balance 0–4–4 type chassis

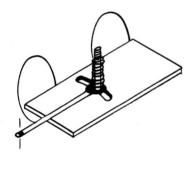

Swing-link bogie with guide arranged simply by cutting semi-circular slot in top of bogie and arranging centre spring screw as a guide. Spring distances bogie from body, pushing body into level position. Adjust by tightening screw.

Simple arrangement using bent wire or strip soldered to bogie to act as spring.

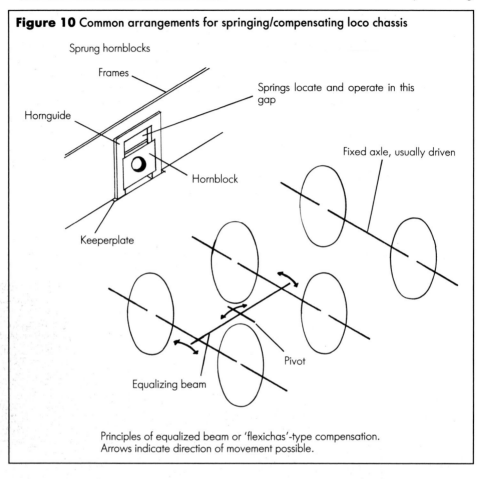

Figure 10 Common arrangements for springing/compensating loco chassis

Sprung hornblocks

Frames

Springs locate and operate in this gap

Hornguide

Fixed axle, usually driven

Hornblock

Keeperplate

Pivot

Equalizing beam

Principles of equalized beam or 'flexichas'-type compensation. Arrows indicate direction of movement possible.

formulated for model railway use, lightly oil the worm and gear wheel, the axles, adjacent bearings and the valve gear joints. Run the loco in each direction on a medium speed setting for half an hour or so, keeping an eye on things. If no continuous track is available, suspend the locomotive chassis from blocks of wood or upside down in a cradle on an improvised test rig. Use oil sparingly, applied on a needle or similar to the exact spot required, and avoid the use of penetrating oils as they may well attack the plastic.

Certain wheel configurations pose some difficulties, in particular the 0–4–4 tank, and this is because of the weight distribution over the bogie wheels. Kit manufacturers provide various solutions to this problem, from complex arrangements to nothing at all, leaving the builder to develop his own. It is not difficult to balance the chassis, and Figure 9 shows how this can be achieved.

There is now an increasing tendency

to incorporate some form of springing or compensation into chassis construction and this is particularly prevalent in etched 4mm scale chassis. The various kit manufacturers offer their own system and the basic principles of the two main types are shown in Figure 10. These systems may be incorporated into the chassis of your loco either by adapting the parts supplied where possible, or by building a new chassis. Milled and profiled mainframes are available for most prototypes from Alan Gibson, and Perseverence Models make a range of chassis kits using the Flexichas principle. Slaters and some Vulcan kits incorporate this feature in O gauge, but the majority of available chassis are rigid. Much has been written on the technicalities of the non-rigid chassis. My own experience proves neither is conclusively better than the other, save for improved current collection which compensation brings. It is a matter of choice.

So far as painting a chassis is con-

A sprung hornblock assembly in an etched chassis kit under construction. This is the other type of 'compensation' referred to and can be compared to the equalizing principle shown in Figure 10. Each wheel is free to move up and down within the limitations of the horn guide.

An overall view of an 0–4–4 chassis based on a solid cast block. The rear bogie is sprung between frame and cross-member and bogie to balance the chassis and prevent the heavy rear end 'sitting down' on the bogie.

cerned, I adopt the following sequence:

1 Paint the mainframes and bogie/pony truck after assembly and after clearances for wheels have been checked and brake hanger fixing points etc drilled.

2 Paint the wheels before final assembly, not forgetting the backs on Romfords in 4mm scale. Cast-iron wheels in O gauge will need blackening.

3 When the chassis is running satisfactorily, touch up the frames and paint the brake hangers, sand boxes and other added details.

4 Where applicable, paint and line the cylinders to match the loco body.

Chapter 5

The body

White metal or cast kits

The manufacturer's intended order of construction outlined in the instruction sheet should be studied and you should identify and be familiar with the parts, choose a prototype and decide on any modifications before construction of the body commences. A dummy run of assembling the parts is recommended, as one of the characteristics of the white metal kit is the need for the builder to prepare the parts for final assembly. This is not as onerous a task as it sounds, and basically consists of cleaning up the parts, removing moulding flash and pips from feeders, and perhaps enlarging locating holes and sockets and trimming parts with a file to as near perfect a fit as possible. Obviously time spent at this stage will not only ease subsequent construction but help to ensure a square, accurate model. Figure 11 shows the method for removal of flash from footplate valances.

In most British and European prototypes (except large tank engines), the

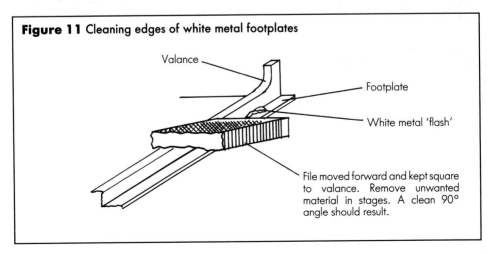

Figure 11 Cleaning edges of white metal footplates

Valance

Footplate

White metal 'flash'

File moved forward and kept square to valance. Remove unwanted material in stages. A clean 90° angle should result.

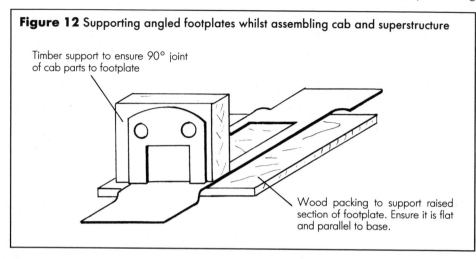

Figure 12 Supporting angled footplates whilst assembling cab and superstructure

Timber support to ensure 90° joint
of cab parts to footplate

Wood packing to support raised
section of footplate. Ensure it is flat
and parallel to base.

footplate is the base around and on to which the other parts are assembled. It is fundamental, therefore, that the footplate is square and true, level and not twisted. A steel straight edge, an engineers' square if available, and, above all, the human eye, will establish this. Careful bending and I mean careful, as white metal snaps easily will achieve a straight edge and remove any twist. It is advisable to check this often as assembly proceeds until the body is sufficiently well advanced to ensure, under normal circumstances, that it will remain flat and true.

It is essential that this squareness of assembly is checked at all stages as construction proceeds. In particular, use the eye and check from all angles. The construction jigs referred to later in Section 3 (Figure 48, page 149), are useful here for assembly of parts such as cab sides and spectacle plates. Simple wooden jigs and improvisation can also help in assembling awkwardly shaped components such as the curved footplates on Gresley locomotives (see Figure 12).

The parts attached to the footplate are often assembled against a shoulder cast in the footplate, and great care should be taken to ensure a good fit and accurate location. The cab, smokebox saddle, etc should be central on the footplate, and when fitting tank sides ensure an equal distance to the edge of the running-plate on each side. Where larger parts such as tank and cab sides and, of course, the footplate itself are not flat, press them down gently on to a flat surface and 'iron' the part flat with the fingers.

As the parts which go over the driving wheels are added to the footplate, particularly the slashers, ensure that they clear the wheels by trying the body on the chassis for clearance as construction progresses.

Where parts contain holes for handrails or to take locating lugs for subsequently added components, it may not be easy to gain access to drill or open these out after they have been fixed in place, therefore ensure that adequate provision is made beforehand.

Buffer beams are usually separate

castings and the locating holes for the buffers and the slots for couplings should be cleaned and the fit checked before they are affixed to the footplate. Also ensure that they are fixed accurately at 90° to the footplate. Sometimes the decoratively shaped corners of footplate valances are separate castings fixed behind the buffer beam, so take care with these to obtain a good fit. Once established and firmly secured, attention with a half-round file and burnishing tool can smooth irregularities. These and other small fiddly bits can often be most easily handled with tweezers rather than our clumsy fingers; and tweezers, unless plastic, do not burn quite so easily either!

Boilers may either be cast in one piece or come in two halves to be assembled by the builder. From time to time, boilers appear which are not at all

In white metal kits, sub-assemblies such as cabs and tank sides can often be made with greater ease than by trying to assemble them on the footplate. The sub-assemblies are fixed to the footplate when complete.

Above *An example of contrast in kit quality. On the left, a standard smokebox door casting, on the right one assembled from etched and turned components.*

Below *Leaving the cab roof off until the last possible moment enables detailing, painting and glazing to take place.*

The footplate casting is the base on which the locomotive superstructure is built and therefore it must be flat. Note the captive nut soldered above the footplate where it will be hidden by the bunker to join the rear securing pivot for the chassis.

round and there is little the builder can do other than return the offending part and seek a replacement. Careful work on the boiler is well repaid, and the one-piece version should be carefully cleaned and prepared. Where boiler halves have to be joined, ensure a smooth joint and, in smoothing down the joint or attending to any slight discrepancies between the two parts, be careful not to file a 'flat'. Check that the boiler sits correctly on the smoke-box saddle, on firebox or cab front and tank sides, in fact any locating point. Ensure also that the boiler and firebox assembly is perfectly in line in both the vertical and horizontal plane, and that it clears the motor, before fixing it in place.

Often the boiler bands cast on the boiler are rather thick and coarse. On the real thing they are in fact only very

thin, and you may wish to reduce their thickness with wet-and-dry paper and files, or even remove them altogether, substituting thin brass sheet ones or merely adding boiler band transfers at the painting stage. I prefer this latter option in 4mm scale.

Despite the manufacturer's instruction, I leave the cab roof off at this stage, although I finish it ready for fixing; this enables glazing and cab detail to be added more easily. I also remove with a knife the cast-in dart or smokebox door handle where this is included, and finish with wet-and-dry paper, substituting a turned brass one. The vulnerable parts, such as whistles, vacuum pipes and steps, are left off for the time being and the body located on the chassis and the whole assembly checked for clearance.

The chimney, dome and safety valves

etc are now added. These must be fixed at 90° from both the front and side views of the boiler, and must of course also be central, in line with each other and carefully seated on the boiler. The half-round file can be used to remove any surplus material from the underside of these parts, and, together with wet-and-dry paper to thin down over-thick flares at their bases. Where boiler fittings are in cast metal, these flared edges can be rolled out using a piece of steel rod (I use an old screwdriver shaft of about ⅛ in diameter) — Figure 13 shows the technique.

At this stage the body should be thoroughly cleaned, excess solder or glue should be removed and it should be burnished and smoothed. Hand-rail knob holes are now drilled (usually No 68 in 4mm scale). Coiled hand-rail wire is usually provided in kits — I have never yet managed to get this perfectly straight, and instead keep in stock a supply of straight hand-rail wire sold by Slaters, Alan Gibson and others. This is usually finer than that supplied in the kits and, together with finer knobs, improves the appearance of the hand-rails. Grab-rails and those hand-rails

Figure 13 Improving the fit of boiler mountings

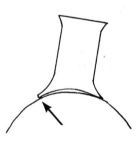

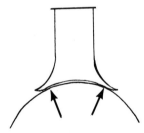

Roll down flares of castings to boiler, moving rod around base of dome and roll downward

Ensure fittings are vertical from front and back, filing where shown if necessary

Careful filing of the underside of the chimney where shown and rolling the edge should result in a good fit. Try rubbing it on tube or dowel the same diameter as the boiler and wrapped in wet and dry.

Figure 14 Bending and fitting hand-rails

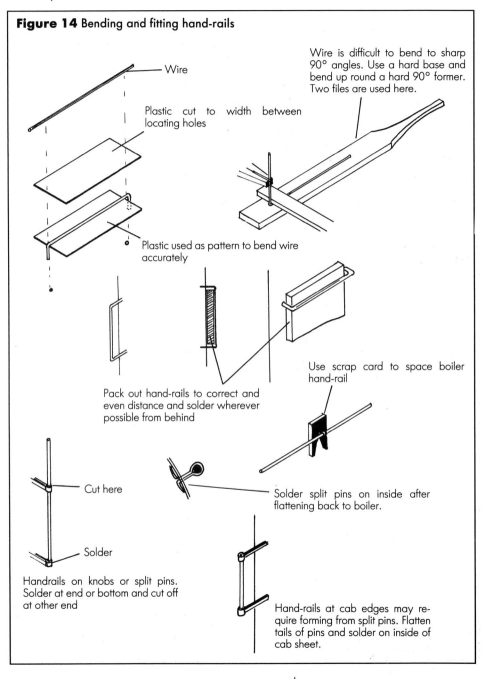

Wire

Plastic cut to width between locating holes

Wire is difficult to bend to sharp 90° angles. Use a hard base and bend up round a hard 90° former. Two files are used here.

Plastic used as pattern to bend wire accurately

Use scrap card to space boiler hand-rail

Pack out hand-rails to correct and even distance and solder wherever possible from behind

Cut here

Solder split pins on inside after flattening back to boiler.

Solder

Handrails on knobs or split pins. Solder at end or bottom and cut off at other end

Hand-rails at cab edges may require forming from split pins. Flatten tails of pins and solder on inside of cab sheet.

Figure 15 Strengthening steps

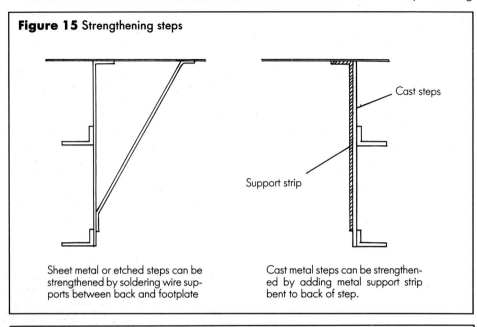

Cast steps

Support strip

Sheet metal or etched steps can be strengthened by soldering wire supports between back and footplate

Cast metal steps can be strengthened by adding metal support strip bent to back of step.

Figure 16 Removable cab roofs

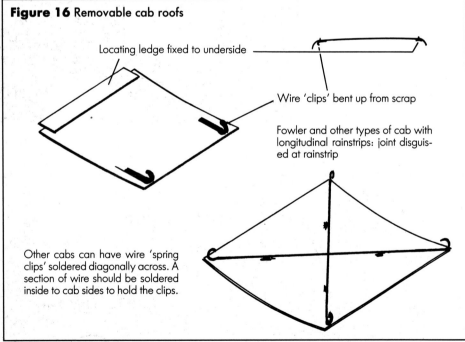

Locating ledge fixed to underside

Wire 'clips' bent up from scrap

Fowler and other types of cab with longitudinal rainstrips: joint disguised at rainstrip

Other cabs can have wire 'spring clips' soldered diagonally across. A section of wire should be soldered inside to cab sides to hold the clips.

which do not have knobs are bent around both ends of a former of scrap material which is the same length as the distance between the two locating holes, the ends of the wire being bent over the former with long nose pliers, as shown in Figure 14.

Any filling of gaps in the main body assembly should now be done with Milliput or a similar filler and allowed to set, then smoothed down before progressing. The body can now be completed and the remaining detail parts added, including the steps, which may benefit from strengthening as shown in Figure 15. Do not fix the cab roof on tank engines, though, unless you do not intend to glaze the windows or detail the cab, until after painting. Alternatively, removable cab roofs could be used, as described in Figure 16. The body should now get a careful inspection: any gaps should be filled, surplus glue, solder or overlooked moulding flash removed and the model cleaned by applying lighter fuel on a cloth. Priming of the body in car aerosol primer will show up any blemishes which may require further filling or sanding. Painting is dealt with in Chapter 6.

Right *The joint of the rear spectacle plate/cabside assembled with low-melt solder.*

Below *A typical 4mm scale white metal loco kit awaiting cleaning up and painting. A first attempt by a 14-year-old.*

Two further views of a cast body under construction as the detail is added to the main body components. The bunker and rear of the cab, already assembled, will be added to the footplate when the detailing of the front of the cab has been completed.

The provision of full cab details is a common feature of more recent kits and is now regarded as the norm in O gauge kits such as the Vulcan AIX shown under construction here.

Etched and sheet metal kits

It is convenient to consider these two types of kit together because the method and principles of construction are similar. Much of what has already been discussed above is also relevant, so the next few paragraphs concentrate on those aspects which vary from the cast kit techniques. The first of these is that the parts will require soldering together, and the second is that for most etched kits the main parts will certainly require removal from a fret and forming from flat into boilers, cab roofs etc. Figure 17 shows various aids and assembly methods for these types of kit, and requires no further comment. The components in etched kits need careful removal from their frets and the easiest method is to 'chisel' the securing tabs through with a stout old knife blade and clean the resultant burr on the components with needle files.

Because there are usually a large number of parts, it is as well to remove them as you require them, particularly the smaller or more delicately detailed parts. It is not possible to have a 'dummy run' assembly of the major components because invariably they will require forming before assembly. It is necessary therefore to adopt a slightly different approach and rely very much on the assembly instructions for an order of assembly, and to take great care that each part is correctly located before it is fixed. You will need to work out problems as you proceed, rather than being able to anticipate them.

If you are not too confident about tackling this type of kit, start with the tender, which is invariably a box, certainly has much less detail than a locomotive and is a good way to ease yourself into the construction. Tender kits are available separately. There are three major problem areas in constructing tenders from this type of kit. Firstly, there is the tender chassis. With any

Figure 17 Assembly aids, etched and sheet metal kits

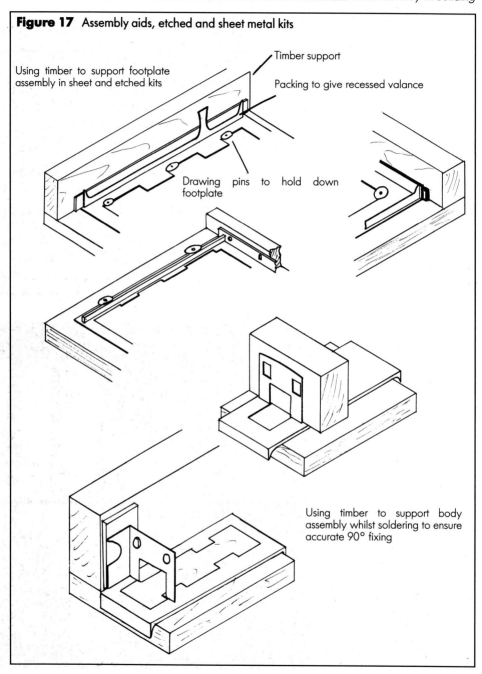

Timber support

Using timber to support footplate assembly in sheet and etched kits

Packing to give recessed valance

Drawing pins to hold down footplate

Using timber to support body assembly whilst soldering to ensure accurate 90° fixing

Chassis and valve gear parts are supplied flat on etched frets, often in nickel silver.

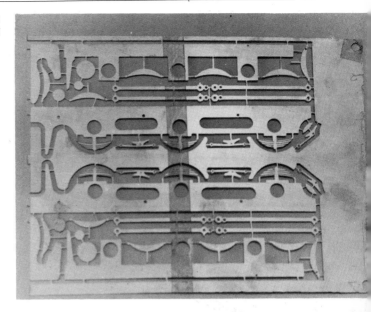

Etched brass kits are also usually supplied flat in frets. The builder must remove the parts carefully and form them into shape. Loco and tender bdies are usually in brass.

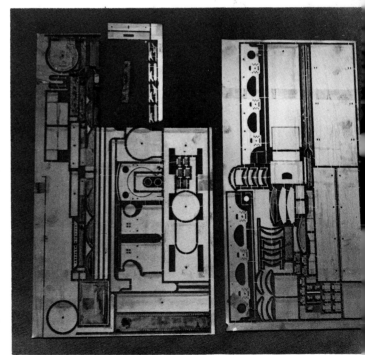

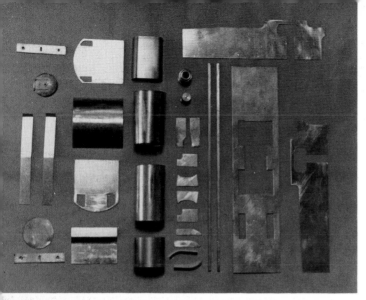

A very basic sheet metal loco kit, which requires a good deal of work by the builder to produce a satisfactory model. This is the traditional type of kit and only one step away from scratch-building.

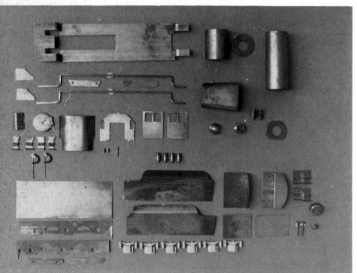

A more sophisticated type of sheet metal kit such as those supplied by Jamieson in 4mm scale and CCW in 7mm scale.

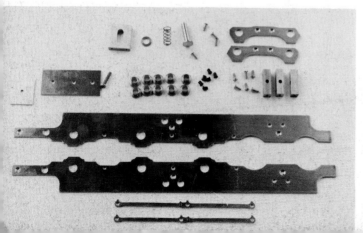

A Vulcan O gauge chassis kit for an LMS 'Jubilee', exquisitely machined and the ideal base for a well-running model, requires only simple screw assembly.

tender, whether cast or from a hard metal kit, do not try to locate the wheels into the tender axle-box castings. It is much easier to make up a set of dummy frames, which, when assembled, are screwed to the underside of the tender footplate or to easily fabricated cross-members which can be fitted to those kits which do not have a continuous tender floor. Most etched kits provide for this kind of chassis, and in O gauge milled chassis are available to provide inside bearing frames for most tenders. The beauty of this system is that you will get a good, square,

well-running tender chassis far more easily than trying to do so using the outside bearing valances/cast axle-boxes. You can also remove the chassis easily for maintenance, and locate brake detail on the inside frames.

The second problem occurs in trying to solder together the tender body from the inside and fixing this to the tender footplate. One answer is to use scrap material, perhaps the waste edge of an etched fret, and solder strips of this between the tender body sides at the bottom of the body $\frac{1}{4}$ in or so in from the end in 4mm scale, $\frac{1}{2}$ in in 7mm

Right *A tender chassis as suggested in the text. Parts for such a chassis may well be included in an etched kit.*

Below *The cross-members between the tender frames are drilled to allow the underframe to be screwed to the tender body.*

Above left *A basic sheet metal tender body shell and separate underframe ready to be assembled as described.*

Left *Although apparently quite basic in detail, a little work and thought provides a well-detailed model. Contrast this picture with the basic shell shown above.*

Above *Outside frames, drag and buffer beams are soldered directly to the tender floor. The holes are for bolts which fix the tender chassis in place.*

Right *The tender frames are first tacked into place and when the builder is happy that they are square and accurately aligned, a fillet of solder is run the length of the joint.*

Further stages in the construction of a tender from an etched kit; the basic shell is completed, etched steps and tool boxes folded up from the flat etchings and soldered in place. All that remains is the fitting of hand-rails, water filler, outside springs, buffers and vacuum pipes before painting.

scale. These strips are drilled in their centres beforehand and either tapped or have a nut soldered on the inside to take the screw which fixes the body to the tender floor or running-plate (the separate assembly of the drag beam, outside frames and buffer beam). To ensure accurate location of the body on the chassis, drill the fixing holes in the tender floor first, where the two strips fastened to the body go, and mark through on to these with a felt marker or matchstick dipped in paint from the underside of the floor when the body is located at its final position. The strips can then be drilled and tapped, and the two assemblies screwed together.

The third difficulty which occurs with many older-type tender sides is the forming of the flared top. Usually, the tender top flares are separate etchings added to the basic box of the tender body which is often half etched down in thickness for a millimetre or so to assist location. It is essential that these components are bent before being soldered to the tender proper. It is far easier to do than to describe. The basic method is to bend the components around a steel rod — an old Meccano axle-rod would suffice. The curved ends which locate on the tender back flare will require trimming; I usually solder the long sides to the tender, and file the rear ends of these pieces as necessary to locate the rear

Figure 18 Simple drawbar assemblies

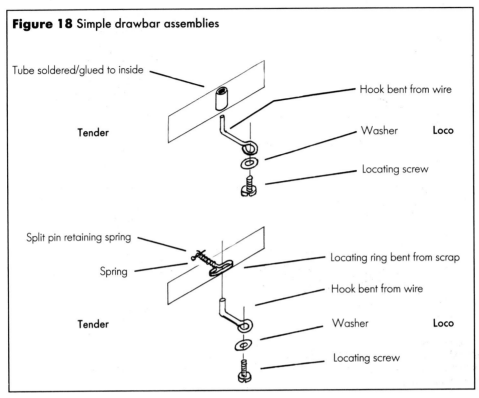

Tube soldered/glued to inside

Hook bent from wire

Tender

Washer   **Loco**

Locating screw

Split pin retaining spring

Locating ring bent from scrap

Spring

Hook bent from wire

Tender

Washer   **Loco**

Locating screw

piece. This, when it fits nicely in the correct position, is soldered in place. Any surplus overhang on the joints can be filed to a smooth finish.

The design of many kits does not go so far as to cover drawbar arrangements between loco and tender. There are possibilities for springing the connecting bar, but I find a simple hook and bar arrangement is quite adequate, and simple suggestions are shown in Figure 18. These unsophisticated but effective and reliable arrangements are easily disguised with the addition of a fall plate between the loco and tender (Figure 19). Remember that if you are using the finished loco on sharp curves, a greater gap between loco and tender will be necessary than on larger radius curves.

As with the white metal kit, the locomotive footplate is the base on which the loco body is built and therefore care needs to be taken to ensure that it is square and true. It will require the addition of valances, buffer beams and any wheel splashers at an early stage. It is essential that the valances are at 90° to the footplate and parallel to the footplate edge. Valances supplied in the kit will either be etchings or square section, and soldering them to the footplate will be made easier by the use of the simple jig arrangement shown in Figure 17, and will ensure a flat footplate.

Some more complex footplates are

Figure 19 Fall plates

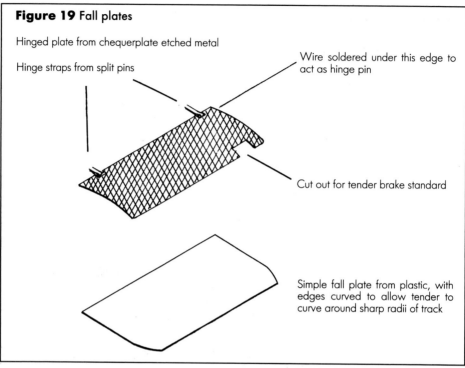

Hinged plate from chequerplate etched metal

Hinge straps from split pins

Wire soldered under this edge to act as hinge pin

Cut out for tender brake standard

Simple fall plate from plastic, with edges curved to allow tender to curve around sharp radii of track

anything but flat, and the assembly of valances to such footplates requires a bit more ingenuity in the provision of packing to support the different heights of the footplate whilst soldering takes place (see Figure 12).

The driving wheel splashers will either be a simple two-part assembly which will require soldering to the footplate, or will require the addition of tops to the splashers sides which fold up from a footplate etching. Figure 20 shows the suggested assembly of these parts, which is, of course, much easier if the splasher tops have been carefully bent to the profile of the sides, particularly important in those splashers which also contain an integral sandbox.

Great care is needed in bending up the splasher sides where they form part

of the footplate component, to avoid distorting the footplate. It is essential that these sides are folded against a strong support on the rest of the footplate which will also help in getting a true 90° fold up. This is easily achieved with a block of wood or even a table edge as shown in the diagram.

It may be necessary to add beading to the splashers, and this can be conveniently represented by soldering on small lengths of square-section brass or nickel, pre-bent to the circumference of the splasher side. The use of a lower melting point solder would aid this and reduce the risk of the splasher top and sides becoming unsoldered as heat is applied to fix the beading.

The location of the splashers on the footplate must be carefully checked, as

Figure 20 Splasher

Bending up splasher sides. Support
footplate with timber and bend up
against this to prevent distortion to
footplate and give an extra bend

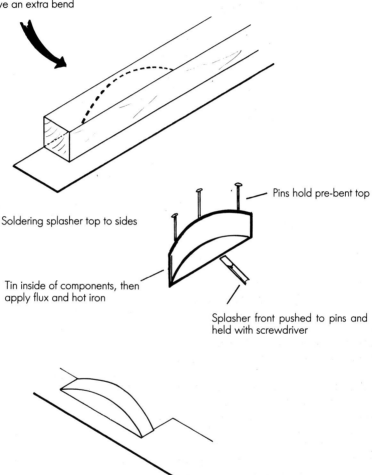

Soldering splasher top to sides

Pins hold pre-bent top

Tin inside of components, then
apply flux and hot iron

Splasher front pushed to pins and
held with screwdriver

Sometimes it is not possible to solder splashers
from inside but usually they can be tacked into
place. Ensure they are vertical and accurately
aligned. Lightly tin footplate and outside bottom of
splasher, flux and apply hot iron just long enough
to fuse solder, otherwise top will come apart. Use
of a lower temperature solder helps to avoid this.

As much soldering as possible should be done underneath inside joints rather than on the outside. The solder inside the splashers and footplate valances can be seen here.

must adequate clearances for the wheels, which should be checked against the already assembled chassis.

Before proceeding further, it is necessary to consider how the chassis is to be fixed to the body and the necessary provision made. Usually two screws are sufficient, one at the front and one at the rear, inserted through the frame spacers into the nuts soldered over the locating holes, in the footplate. The boiler and firebox usually locate at the front of the footplate and on the cab front spectacle plate respectively. For this reason I usually build up two separate assemblies, the smokebox/boiler/firebox, and the cab.

The cab sides and roof may be in one piece or be built up from separate pieces, depending on the design of the kit and the peculiarities of the prototype. If separate pieces require soldering together to form the cab, or a flat etching needs to be bent to shape, add detail such as beading around the windows beforehand whilst the parts are still flat. Figure 21 shows the method using tinned wire or section sweated to the cabsides.

Where cabs, or indeed other sections, are formed by bending the etched sheet, it is usual for the design to incorporate half-etched fold lines on the back of the part where the bend is required. Take care in forming these bends and use a good solid support held steadily in the vice and a block of wood or steel bar to bend the component. Use a support and bending aid longer than the component, and employ a steady even pressure to form the correct angle. Bends in larger components such as cab or tank sides can be improvised quite easily by placing the larger section of the component .on a flat solid surface, for example a table or worktop edge, and holding this in place with a block of wood along the fold lines; a second piece is then applied to

Detail is substantially completed and, as suggested in the text, it is easier to keep the model 'cleaned up' as work progresses.

Figure 21 Fixing beading

Cab beading

Tack into place at end

Lightly tin inside of beading and edge of cab sheet

Bend and hold beading to cab side, gradually moving down as soldered.

Pre-curved beading

Square cab windows

Beading pre–bent and held in place with pins. Fix as above.

Office staples are useful and available in various sizes, one of which may be suitable.

Soldering straight beading such as on tender sides

Wire and edge tinned

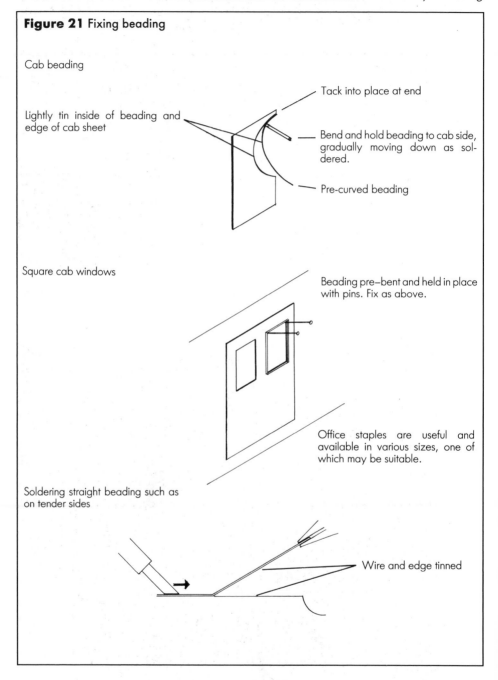

Above *Beading sweated on to the edges as described and shown in figure 21 is clearly shown in this view.*

Below *Another view of the sheet metal tender showing the detailed front end.*

Beading along tank and bunker top edges and around cab sides is a characteristic feature of many locomotives, and has been fitted here as described in the text. The holes which can be seen will locate, in the way of the actual locomotive, the cab handrails.

the other part of the component which is bent downwards over the edge. There will be occasions when the fold required is not at an acute angle, but more of a curve, such as cab roofs. In such circumstances, improvisation is the key, the component being bent round a suitable former, perhaps a piece of dowelling, broom handle or steel rod. Careful manipulation with finger and thumb will produce the correct shape. If you are bending some of the thinner etched materials, take great care and try and achieve the correct shape the first time, as subsequent straightening and

correcting of any fold or curve will almost certainly leave blemish on the surface from distortion.

Usually, cab backheads and details are left until later, and for this purpose, where design allows, I usually leave the fixing of the cab roof until a later stage, and with tank locos until after painting, if possible, to allow for detailing the cab, particularly important in O gauge.

The cab unit can be put aside until the firebox/boiler/smokebox has been assembled. It will, however, need to be fixed to the footplate assembly at a later stage. If no specific instructions are

Above *A cab roof formed from flat around a suitable round object. The boiler and smokebox wrapper have been formed round a broom handle.*

Below *An underside view of a simple etched loco kit showing the assembled valances and buffer beams which were held using jigs as shown in Figure 17 whilst being soldered.*

A selection of castings are usually provided to finish etched kits. These are the parts which cannot be conveniently etched.

With open cab locomotives it is worthwhile adding some representation of cab detail. The balsa wood floor hides the captive nut which takes the rear chassis locating screw.

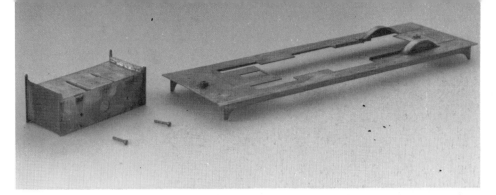

Above *This etched brass locomotive body is designed to have the main body constructed in sub-assemblies, which are bolted to the footplate, as discussed in the text. Here the bunker and footplate are shown.*

Right *A further sub-assembly in this kit is the tank sides, spectacle plate and firebox top.*

provided, there are a number of ways this can be achieved. Soldering directly to the footplate is one, while another is to provide a strip of metal soldered across the bottom of the cab between the sides. This can be drilled and thinned down, and 10 BA nuts soldered over the holes drilled in the cross-piece to enable bolts to be passed through the underside of the footplate to hold the cab in place. The captive nuts can be hidden by the addition of a cab floor made from balsa scored to represent planking.

Where no specific instructions or method are suggested or designed into the kit, then the tank, bunker and cab assembly, on a side tank loco, can usually be similarly assembled as a unit separate from the footplate. Again, suitably placed cross-strips, towards the tank front, bunker centre and either side of the cab, say, are used to fix these sub-assemblies together. An advantage of this arrangement of separate assemblies is the ability to break down the body for easier detailing or painting and lining — particularly important where more complex liveries are used.

The next job to be tackled is the assembly of the firebox, boiler and smokebox. In most cases, I find it convenient to form these separately, fix them together and then fix this as a further sub-assembly to the footplate/cab assemblies.

Fireboxes come in two basic types. The round-topped variety is usually for

Above *Early stages in the assembly of a sheet metal body kit.*

Left *Smokeboxes are often built up with wrappers formed around the boiler barrel. The turned brass boiler here has the smokebox wrapper formed from thin sheet, the rivets having been punched out from the inside. The assembly is designed to also form the smokebox saddle into which the boiler tube is a push fit.*

model purposes an extension of the boiler barrel and is often incorporated in that part with additional flared pieces added between the 'barrel' and the running-plate to form the firebox sides. This arrangement is common where the boiler is made from a pre-formed and machined brass tube. Where the boiler is rolled from flat, these firebox sides are usually formed by the simple expedient of not rolling the firebox section completely round. Be careful when forming the sides of these round-topped fireboxes, as the shape varies from being vertical to curving inwards before dropping vertically down to fit between the frames. Check with the drawings and photographs, because the subtlety of this shape helps to add to the character of the prototype.

Belpaire fireboxes come in various subtle shapes too, and usually some

Figure 22 Fireboxes

Belpaire, Midland type. (Construction principle applies to all types of Belpaire box except on Stainer and Bulleid (rebuilt) 'Pacifics'

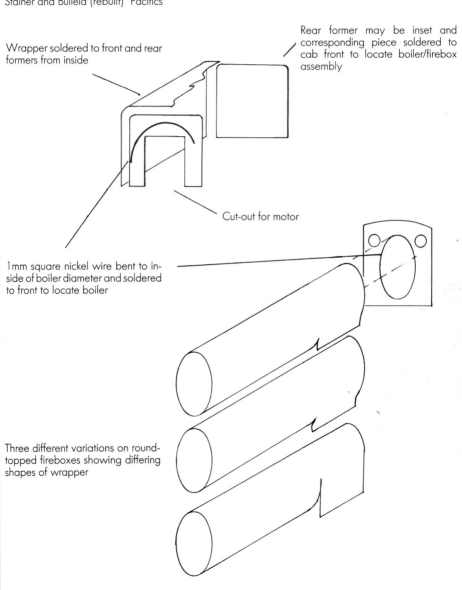

Wrapper soldered to front and rear formers from inside

Rear former may be inset and corresponding piece soldered to cab front to locate boiler/firebox assembly

Cut-out for motor

1mm square nickel wire bent to inside of boiler diameter and soldered to front to locate boiler

Three different variations on round-topped fireboxes showing differing shapes of wrapper

Figure 23 Rolling a sheet metal or etched boiler

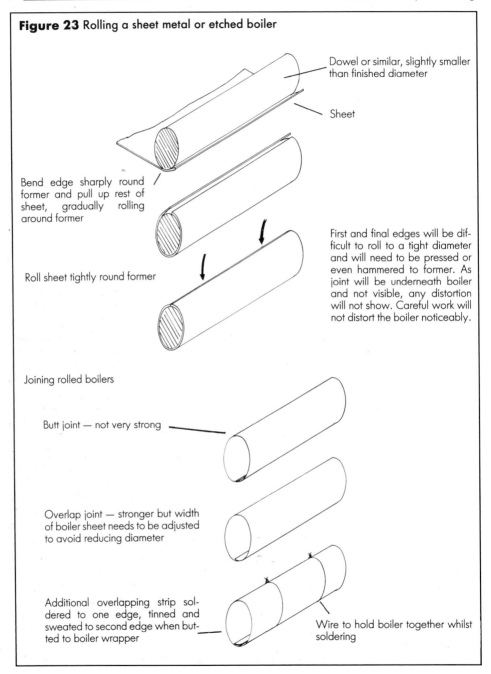

Dowel or similar, slightly smaller than finished diameter

Sheet

Bend edge sharply round former and pull up rest of sheet, gradually rolling around former

First and final edges will be difficult to roll to a tight diameter and will need to be pressed or even hammered to former. As joint will be underneath boiler and not visible, any distortion will not show. Careful work will not distort the boiler noticeably.

Roll sheet tightly round former

Joining rolled boilers

Butt joint — not very strong

Overlap joint — stronger but width of boiler sheet needs to be adjusted to avoid reducing diameter

Additional overlapping strip soldered to one edge, tinned and sweated to second edge when butted to boiler wrapper

Wire to hold boiler together whilst soldering

Figure 23 continued

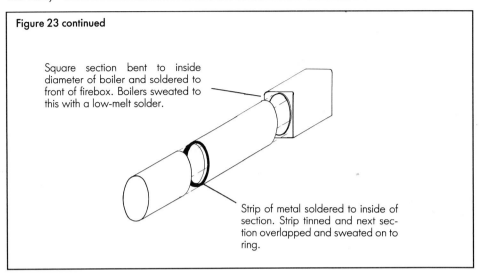

Square section bent to inside diameter of boiler and soldered to front of firebox. Boilers sweated to this with a low-melt solder.

Strip of metal soldered to inside of section. Strip tinned and next section overlapped and sweated on to ring.

former is provided for the firebox wrapper, even if this is only a front and back. It is essential to check the shape of these formers and their overall dimensions. Even where the wrapper is formed, great care needs to be taken to ensure the correct shape before final assembly. Do not just assume that the parts are correct — check at all stages of assembly. Figure 22 shows the assembly method. It is essential that the firebox is square and true, so take your time and go for accuracy.

Boiler barrels, if not supplied as a machined tube, may well require forming, particularly in etched kits. Ideally a rolling mill should be used, but, with care, we can improvise and carefully form thin boiler etchings around a surface of a suitable diameter — a broom handle, say. The boiler will be supported on formers which may be brass washers or etchings. These are soldered to the inside of the boiler as shown in Figure 23. Ensure that these are true and square, thus avoiding any twist in

the boiler. In a taper boiler, the smokebox, which is parallel is usually a separate piece from the tapered boiler barrel. These pieces, formed as outlined above for parallel boilers, are usually joined together by an interior 'ring' which crosses the joint and to which both sections are soldered.

The smokebox, particularly on parallel-boilered locomotives, is often of a greater diameter than the boiler barrel, and is often represented by an additional wrapper, usually incorporating rivet and other surface detail. This smokebox wrapper is carefully formed to just go over the boiler, and is either tinned and sweated into place, or can be fastened with a thin coating of epoxy resin. The wrapper can be held in place on the former as the boiler barrel (Figure 23). When fixing an etched smokebox wrapper, ensure that any holes for fixing the chimney etc which may be in the boiler and wrapper are aligned.

The smokebox/boiler and firebox sec-

Figure 24 Methods of fixing boiler/smokebox assembly at smokebox end

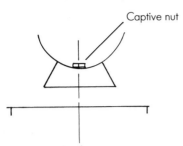

Captive nut

Captive nut soldered inside smokebox. Smokebox saddle soldered to smokebox and assembly bolted to footplate.

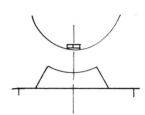

Saddle soldered to footplate from inside and smokebox bolted to saddle.

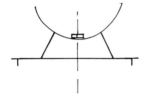

Saddle soldered to smokebox and smokebox to saddle. Nut used for front chassis locating screw.

tions should now be fixed together, by either soldering or using epoxy resin adhesive. It is essential that the whole of this assembly is square, true and equidistant from the footplate edges. Ensure this by constant reference to the footplate assembly as construction progresses. (figure 23).

Some form of smokebox saddle will be provided, either from a casting or to be made up as part of the footplate, which may also incorporate frame extensions and valve covers. Ensure that the smokebox sits squarely and snugly on the saddle and holds the boiler assembly at the correct height. Remedy any problems here by filing the saddle to fit the smokebox.

Provision can now be made to fix this sub-assembly to the rest of the model.

Soldering is usual, from inside the firebox to the cab spectacle plate. This is quite easy, as the footplate is usually open to accommodate the motor. The fixing at the smokebox end can be arranged by drilling through from beneath the footplate and either tapping the smokebox 8 or 10 BA, or soldering a nut on the underside of the smokebox in front of the pre-drilled hole, where the saddle is hollow. Figure 24 illustrates this. Alternatively, the saddle can be soldered to the boiler from the outside, but carefully to prevent other parts from coming loose and to help maintain its appearance.

The boiler assembly can have the holes for the hand-rail knobs drilled at this stage, along with holes for boiler feed clacks, lubricators, ejectors, whist-

Figure 25 Lamp brackets

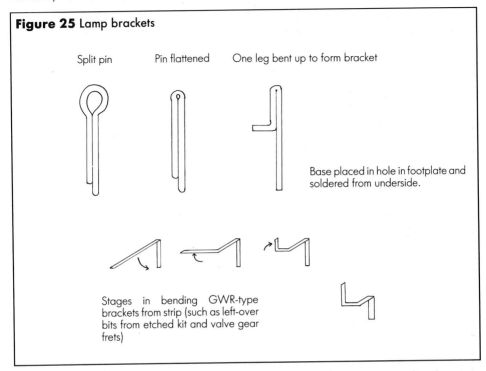

Split pin   Pin flattened   One leg bent up to form bracket

Base placed in hole in footplate and soldered from underside.

Stages in bending GWR-type brackets from strip (such as left-over bits from etched kit and valve gear frets)

le, safety valves, etc. Similarly, before final assembly of the boiler unit to the footplate, it will be found more convenient to drill the footplate to locate sandbox fillers, hand-rails, lamp brackets, reversing rods, etc. Figure 25 shows how lamp brackets can be formed.

The cab can now be detailed and this, I consider, is essential in 7mm scale models, and desirable and quite possible in 4mm scale. Many of the more recent kits include at least a representation of the backhead, whilst some provide the fullest details. The Vulcan AIX cab shown under construction is an example of the latter approach.

It is a straightforward matter to detail a basic cast backhead using scrap material, and Figure 26 shows how this might be done. Where no backhead is provided, it is more than likely that a suitable cast one can be found. Whilst, strictly speaking, the cabs of individual locomotives vary, for most purposes a general representation will suffice. If a cast backhead is not available, it is a simple matter to fabricate one from plasticard as shown in the diagram. Cab floors are easily fabricated and fitted; I use ⅛ in balsa sheet, scored to represent planking, in O gauge and 1/32 in sheet in 4mm scale. The balsa can be stained and coloured with washes of black/brown paint. Fall plates can be added and chequer plate material is available suitable for use in both 4mm and 7mm scales. It is essential that the plate allows free movement between loco and tender and consequently for most

Figure 26 Cab detailing

Cab backheads are easily made from plasticard

(a) shows a backhead made from plasticard section covered with an outer skin of sheet. It should, of course, match the firebox profile at the cab end.
(b) a round-topped boiler laminated from sheet/plastic. Two layers of 60 thou should do for most 4mm locomotives.

Round edge with wet-and-dry skin

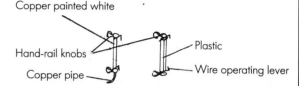

Plastic section frame

On older locomotives, wrap copper wire (thick) round outer edge

Washout plugs from slivers of square section

Cut hole for firehole or simply add door from 10/thou

(a)   (b)

Firehole doors and levers can be made from thin sheet metal or plastic, and strip used for levers and runners

Copper painted white

Hand-rail knobs

Copper pipe

Plastic

Wire operating lever

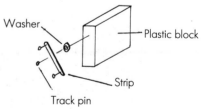

Water gauge made from hand-rail knobs and plastic or copper wire painted white

Regulator

Washer or disc

Track pin

Handle from bent wire

Screw reverse

Washer

Plastic block

Strip

Track pin

Gauges

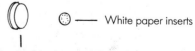

Brass washers of different diameters sweated together for small gauges

White paper inserts

'Top hat' bush, edge filed thin to take large diameter gauges

Figure 26 continued

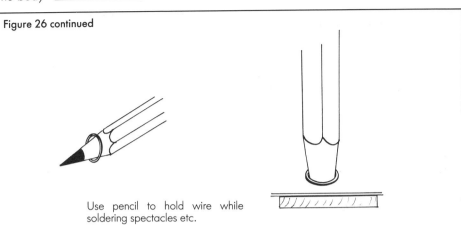

Use pencil to hold wire while soldering spectacles etc.

Below *Cab detailing under way with a fall plate, backhead and cab beadng in place. Cleaning up and filling has yet to take place. The holes in the cab side will locate folding windshields.*

Above *Loco body detailing with parts fabricated from scrap sheet metal and brass rod and wire.*

Below *Cylinders and valve gear on an LMS Class '5'.*

This rear three-quarter view shows the cab detail to good effect. This model is built from a kit intended to provide a round-top-boiler locomotive of the pre-war era. The boiler, smokebox, above footplate frame extensions and cab details have been modified to give a locomotive in its final form. The text refers both to the need to choose a particular locomotive to model and the possibilities of modifying kits to give models of class variants or locomotives at different periods.

model railways it is necessary to compromise to achieve this. The simplest way is to curve the edge which fits over the tender. Alternatively, if your layout has generous curves it may simply be a matter of making the plate a little narrower than the prototype. The fall plate is usually fixed to the loco cab and whilst it is quite possible to arrange for this to be hinged, all that is necessary is to glue or solder the plate in place.

Take advantage also of the many alternative parts which are available to improve or detail your loco. The illustrations show a sample of the different qualities of components available and how simple substitution with better, or sometimes more accurate, parts than those supplied with the kit can improve its appearance no end. No major work is usually involved; it is just a question of seeking visual rather than dimensional fidelity in most cases and not accepting as of right that the compo-

A selection of detailing components for 4 mm scale available for the more discerning modeller and often better than those supplied with the kit. Their use can make a considerable difference to the overall appearance of the model.

This locomotive is based on a K's white metal kit but, as suggested in the text, has been transformed with relative ease by the substitution of certain key parts. For example, turned brass Salter valves, safety valve cover and boiler feed clacks have been added. Brakes, rodding and linkages have been added and the wheels supplied have been substituted by Maygib correct pattern wheels of much finer profile.

nents supplied are the best to represent that feature.

It is, however, often difficult to judge from advertisements in the model press whether a particular part will improve your model or not. There is a truly vast range of bits and pieces on the market, of superior quality rather than run-of-the-mill, and it is unlikely that your model shop will have more than a few items in stock. Model railway exhibi-

tions are increasingly *the* source for seeing such specialist products because many specialist manufacturers and traders attend. G. Norton, Model Engineers, 100 Thorne Road, Doncaster, and Crownline Models, 8 Rame Terrace, Rame Cross, Penyryn, Cornwall, are two useful and reliable sources of such parts and produce extensive lists of parts for detailing and improving models.

CHAPTER 6
Painting and lining

It is often said that a good paint job can improve an ordinary model beyond recognition. Assuming that the model is true, square and well finished, this is undoubtedly true. It will not, however, make a model with an inaccurate, badly assembled chassis run better, nor make the proverbial silk purse out of a sow's ear. The reverse, though, is true, and many otherwise excellent models are ruined by a poor paint finish.

So, if you have achieved a squarely assembled model which runs to your satisfaction, how do you achieve a good paint finish? The notes which follow are intended to guide you to a competent and acceptable finish.

There are two basic requirements for the achievement of an acceptable paint finish. One is the preparation of the model, ie ensuring that any blemishes are filled and smoothed, excess solder, glue or filler is removed and the model is thoroughly cleaned of grease, dust, flux, etc. So far as cleaning is concerned, rather than be faced with a significant and sometimes difficult and awkward job (and thus heighten the temptation to rush preparation in order to get a finished model sooner), I clean up soldered joints as they are made, largely with old knife blades and broken files which I use as scrapers, finishing off with wet and dry paper or a fibreglass burnishing tool. I do not bother cleaning up joints inside the model providing that a) they cannot be seen and b) they do not impair the fit of the body to the chassis or mar the movement of the bogies and valve gear. Any flux, filings or grease, however, must be removed.

Once the model is filled and excess solder removed, I give it a quick rub over with the burnishing tool. This is particularly important with white metal kits. I then wash off any flux or grease with lighter fuel applied on a cotton pad. A photographer's lens-cleaning brush is handy to dust the model immediately before priming.

Cellulose primer sold in aerosol cans as car touch-up paint is all that I use for priming metal. The cans are quite cheap and each will spray several models. The can should be thoroughly shaken and light, even coats of primer applied, building up the coverage evenly and allowing it to dry between coats (this paint is sufficiently dry to re-coat after a few minutes). Once the top side of the body is covered, turn it on its side and

Above *The completed model awaiting final cleaning, filling and painting.*

Below *A K's OO gauge white metal kit almost ready for the paint shop.*

prime the underside thoroughly. I should perhaps add that once the model is cleaned and prepared for painting, it should be handled as little as possible. There is an obvious need to move the locomotive around whilst spraying to get an even coat; the improvised arrangement shown in Figure 27 has served me well.

The primed model should now be examined closely, but handled as little as possible, and any imperfections in the surface dealt with. The primer will show these up more than the unprimed surface did, and show them more clearly as there is no reflection to deflect our critical eye.

When you are happy with the finish, consideration can be given to the final coat. The choice of livery is clearly up to the builder and if earlier advice on choosing to model a particular loco at a given period has been followed, no doubt the livery will also have been determined by how the model was detailed at that time. There is now so much information available that major inaccuracies are inexcusable, even though there may be some doubt about the finer details of liveries. The books listed in Appendix I are good sources of information.

There are well-matched paints for a significant number of railway colours available in aerosol cans and in small tinlets which can be used thinned in an airbrush. Alternatively, that good old stand-by, the car touch-up paint aerosol can, is available in such a wide range of colours that a fair approximation of the colour needed is almost certainly available. Colour perception is a very personal matter, and as long as you're happy that the colour you've chosen is right, then it's your model. If you use the matched paints, this problem should not arise.

Perhaps the most common colour for locomotives is black, and here again recourse to car touch-up aerosol can be

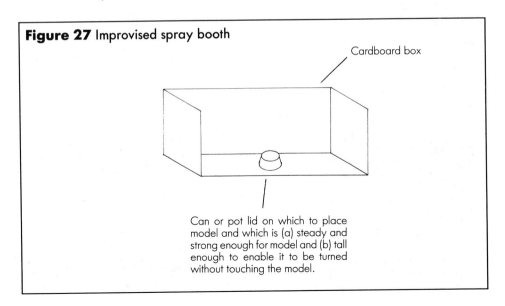

Figure 27 Improvised spray booth

Cardboard box

Can or pot lid on which to place model and which is (a) steady and strong enough for model and (b) tall enough to enable it to be turned without touching the model.

made. Matt black touch-up paint is used, even in O gauge, as a high gloss finish just does not look right on small-scale models. This matt black paint is actually not a dead matt but has a slight sheen to it if applied under normal temperature conditions, just about right in my view for the model loco-motive. There are also other advantages in using this paint. In particular, being cellulose based it dries very hard and it is touch dry within minutes, thus mini-mizing contamination from that old enemy, dust. Lining can be carried out with enamel paints and any unsatisfac-tory work removed without damaging the cellulose base colour. It is, however, essential to use this paint in a well-ventilated room and away from any naked flame or heating elements.

Without doubt, however, the best finish is obtained with an airbrush and, if you are intending to build a lot of kits, it is a worthwhile investment. I have to

This enlarged view shows two common faults, which are visible even at normal size and which, with careful preparation before painting as detailed in the text, can be avoided. The unsightly blob at the top of the grab handle is excessive superglue which should have been removed at primer stage with a sharp knife, while the hole at the bottom could have been filled.

be honest and admit to favouring the touch-up aerosol, even though I have both airbrush and spray gun. But, as I said at the outset, you develop your own favourite approaches and techniques and your own favoured materials and tools as you gain experience. I would not however, recommend brush painting other than for small areas as it is difficult to get a finish comparable to a sprayed one.

Whether you use an airbrush or an aerosol, the basic techniques are the same. Light, even coats are required, building up the finish stage by stage rather than trying to cover in one coat. Keep the spray at a reasonable distance from the model and move the spray evenly and horizontally along its length. It is of paramount importance that the spray is kept moving and not allowed to stop at all, otherwise an uneven coating will result. Start the movement just before and finish just after the model.

Buffer beams can be painted with a brush and matt paint. Ensure that the paint is thoroughly stirred before use, and is applied in thin, even coats from a clean, good quality, preferably sable, brush. Similarly, other detail can be painted, such as, in other than black locos, the smokebox, footplate splasher tops, etc.

If the model requires lining out, once the top coat and details are painted you can consider how best to achieve this. Basically, it is a choice between transfers or hand lining. Transfers come in a variety of colours and styles, covering the main liveries of the British railway companies. They will be of two basic types, waterslide or dry print (the rub-on type), and should be applied in accordance with manufacturer's rec-

ommendations. There are now a number of preparations available from your model shop to help transfers to settle down over rivet and similar surface detail, and to dissolve corner film on waterslide transfers. I find 4mm scale lining transfers excellent in most cases for 7mm scale applications, particularly the usually coarser waterslide type. With waterslide transfers, despite the fact that the directions suggest that it is not necessary, I always cut them carefully with a new fine blade, right up to the design.

Waterslide transfers have the advantage of being easy to adjust and move, very useful with lining, particularly with boiler-band lining which will have to be slid under hand-rails and other details. With these it is easier to apply them if they are cut to length before soaking and taken to the model still on their carrying layer, being put into the approximate place, the carrying layer removed from under the design and the transfer adjusted into its final position.

Dry print or rub-on transfers cannot easily be adjusted and must be applied in their final position. This is not an onerous task on plain sides, but where complicated curved or narrow edges, such as footplate valances or wheel splashers, must be lined, it is easier to cut the design needed from the sheet or to release the design on to glass and transfer this to the model. On panelling such as tender sides, I mark the corners with a soft pencil, add the corner transfers first and then fill in the straight lines.

Beware with rub-on transfers that the paint does not peel from the surface as the backing sheet is withdrawn. It helps to prevent this if the transfer is partly released by rubbing over the backing

The almost completed model shown under construction in earlier pictures. Glazing has yet to be added to the cab spectacle plate and sand pipes to the chassis. The latter are quite delicate and I always arrange to fit these last, supergluing into pre-drilled holes, pipes bent to shape from wire.

sheet before it is applied to the model. It is, of course, essential that the paint on the model has hardened thoroughly before the lining transfers are added. I prefer to put the model on one side in a box to prevent dust getting to it for at least a week after painting, even with cellulose paint.

Hand lining is by no means as difficult as it sounds and, like any other model work, practice is the key to good results. The draughtsman's spring bow-pen is the best tool for the job and is not difficult to use (see Figure 44, page 139). The spring is tightened to thin the line

drawn and slackened off to widen it. New paint only should be used, thoroughly mixed and thinned if necessary to a consistency which will allow it to flow from the pen evenly without flooding. The bow-pen is tightened and paint is added from a cocktail stick between the spring blades and up to a maximum of $\frac{1}{4}$ in up the blades. The blades are then opened until the correct thickness of line is achieved–practise on scrap material. Lining can then commence on the model. The pen must be kept vertical at all times to ensure an even flow of paint from the point of the blades. Try to finish a complete line with one fill of the pen rather than run out of paint half-way through; experience will show how much you can do with the paint left in the pen before it runs out. To refill the pen, clean it out thoroughly with thinners, stir the paint left and continue lining.

It is quite feasible to line large panels such as tender sides with the aid of a template as shown in Figure 28. Basically, a plasticard template is cut, the edges smoothed and the corners curved accurately if appropriate, and this is held in the correct position on the model with small pieces of Blu-Tack in each corner and drawn round with a pen. Try the template out on scrap first to ensure the correct shape and that sufficient smoothness of edge has been achieved to let the pen pass round easily.

If you build several models, eventually a set of templates can be built up and it is useful to label them for future use, such as 'BR mixed traffic livery — Red line Fowler 3,500 gallon tender side'. Multi-coloured lining can easily be built up using templates successively smaller than the previous one, starting with the outside line first.

To line the model successfully, it is important that it is held still and that there is some means of supporting the ruler when straight lines are drawn. The arrangement shown in Figure 45 is adequate for this purpose. For 'one off' jobs you could improvise with heavy books.

There are many lettering transfers available, and their application calls for little comment other than to ensure that the rows of numbers and lettering are applied level and vertical, not as easy or as obvious as it sounds. The best aid to this is a pencil line which can be used as a base line for the lettering.

When you are happy with the paint finish, a coat of varnish can be applied to protect the lining and lettering. The mini-sprays available from Humbrol provide a range of alternative finishes from dead matt to high gloss. I prefer a satin finish applied in light coats as previously discussed for the primer and the top coat. Next paint the cab interior; the top half is usually a light buff or cream colour and the bottom half black or brown. Pick out the gauges and

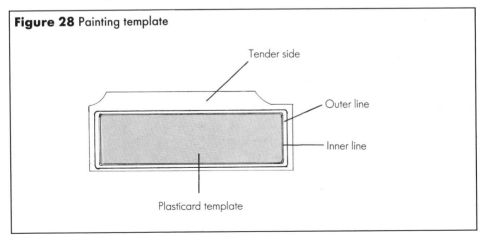

Figure 28 Painting template

Tender side

Outer line

Inner line

Plasticard template

Above *Earlier liveries were often quite ornate but few could have been as striking as the LNWR lined livery applied to this GEM kit by a bow-pen as described.*

Below *An ex-LSWR Adams Radial completed and painted.*

pipework in brass and copper, and paint the faces of the gauges white. Buffer heads should be dark grey with a dark smudged centre, and the shanks painted silver to represent the polished steel from the continual pressing into their housings.

All that is left now is to add the finishing details, such as coal in the tender or bunker — and here there is no substitute for the real thing. I use crushed coal, moulded into the shape desired and held in place with slightly diluted PVA woodwork glue applied with an eye-dropper. Add lamps — there are several cast ones available from Springside together with locomotive tool sets, fire irons, etc — and do not forget to add some spilt coal around the tender front footplate, near the coal plate or around the tender top near the water fillers. If you do not want lamps fixed to your loco, place some on the footplate; the GWR often had spare lamps carried on brackets there. Spare lamps might be carried on the tender front near the lockers and locomotive tools can be added here. Perhaps also add a slacking pipe over the cabsides made from fine wire insulation tube. Last but not least, don't forget the crew!

SECTION II
Rolling-stock

This section deals with the construction of rolling-stock. There is now a considerable choice of rolling-stock, goods, passenger and special service vehicles, available in kit form. They come in a variety of materials from the simple plastic kit to more complex etched metal varieties, the best of which produce showcase models.

The conveyance of goods was, for most railway companies, far more important in revenue terms than the carriage of passengers. It is fitting, therefore, that the humble goods wagon has been taken more seriously in recent years, both by the railway historian and the modeller. As a result there are now several excellent publications detailing the goods stock of various railway companies and BR, which provide drawings, photographs and other details such as numbering and modification/rebuild details, essential for accurate models. A selection of these publications is listed in the Appendix.

Goods stock is a significant element in helping to provide the correct 'feel' and authenticity on a model railway. The great variety, not only of types, but also styles, colouring, condition and detail to be found in the pre-modernization goods train can only be reproduced authentically by the judicious use of kit-built vehicles. Nevertheless, some of the ideas on painting, detailing and finishing can equally be applied with good effect to ready-to-run models.

Coaches are in themselves fascinating vehicles, displaying in their design and interior style and decor not only the skills of their designers but also the developing trends in production and engineering techniques, reflecting the social attitudes of their day. The types of accommodation and facilities provided (or not, as the case may be) for various classes of passengers clearly reflected this. More importantly, the style and decor of passenger vehicles reflected the hopes and ambitions of the times, the solidness of Victorian design with its fussiness of detail giving way to Edwardian elegance and the new times of Art Deco.

Coaching stock of the various railway companies was often very distinctive, showing a family likeness and evolution of design, but quite definitely identifying it as belonging to a particular company. As with goods stock, but perhaps more obviously, the model passenger train is very important in creating authenticity and must reflect reality. Despite the tremendous increase in the number of accurate ready-to-run models in recent years, even with 4mm scale it will be necessary to tap the vast range of kits available for coaching stock. Again, as with the wagons, many of the ideas in the ensuing pages could be used with advantage in detailing and improving ready-to-run items.

CHAPTER 7
Wagons

The railway modeller is now served with a considerable and growing range of rolling-stock kits, particularly in 4mm and 7mm scales. In 7mm scale, recourse to kit building for rolling-stock is now essential, there being no currently available ready-to-run range except for a few European and North American types.

The materials used in rolling-stock kits are plastic, white metal, etched brass and, sometimes for coaches, pre-formed and punched aluminium.

Plastic kits

The basic construction of plastic coach and wagon kits calls for little comment, as the essentials discussed previously with regard to locomotives are equally important in rolling-stock construction.

Squareness is essential, and so is a flat floor for wagons and coaches to avoid a twisted underframe and consequent poor running. Square assembly is again aided by the use of the wooden blocks and supports as shown in Figure 29. Careful preparation is necessary to ensure the correct fit of parts and great care is needed, particularly with fine underframe parts, when cutting them from their sprues. A *sharp*, fine blade is required and for the finest of parts I have used single-edged razor blades, used with holders available from graphic art shops. There are occasions when the finest parts have moulding flash, and great care is needed in

A selection of wagons from the high-quality Slaters range.

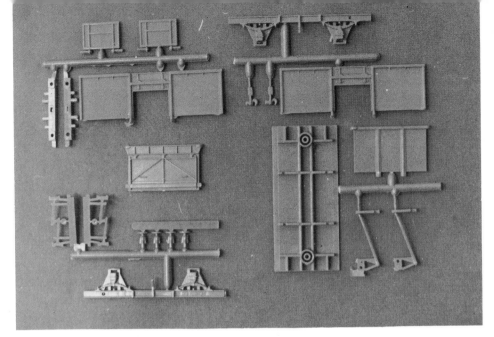

Above *Typical components of a simple 4mm scale wagon kit.*

Below *Many American plastic freight vehicle kits come with the main body shell pre-painted and lettered. A kit from the Roundhouse range, typical of this style, is shown here.*

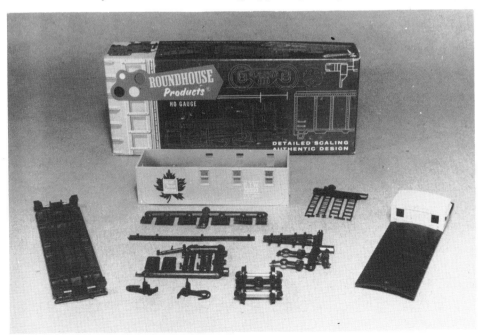

Figure 29 Wooden blocks to aid square and accurate assembly

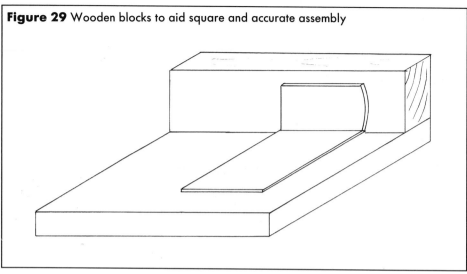

Figure 30 Replacing moulded plastic hand-rails

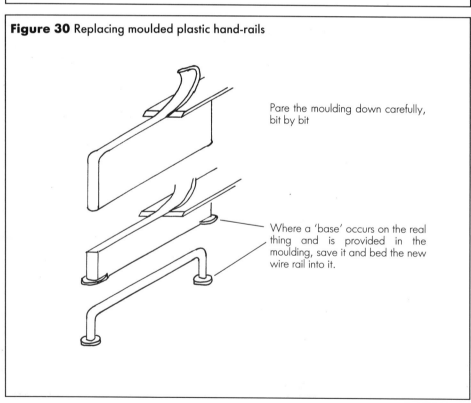

Pare the moulding down carefully, bit by bit

Where a 'base' occurs on the real thing and is provided in the moulding, save it and bed the new wire rail into it.

Figure 31 Fixing windows to plastic-bodied vehicles

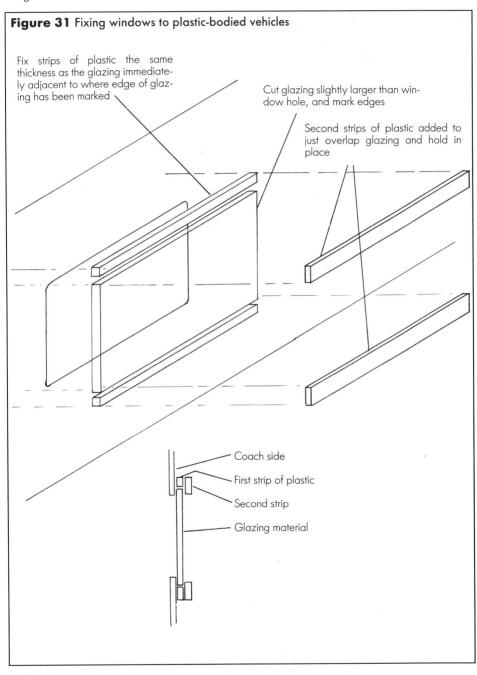

Fix strips of plastic the same thickness as the glazing immediately adjacent to where edge of glazing has been marked

Cut glazing slightly larger than window hole, and mark edges

Second strips of plastic added to just overlap glazing and hold in place

Coach side

First strip of plastic

Second strip

Glazing material

removing this to avoid breaking the part itself.

Even if you have no intention of modifying the basic kit, there are some easily achieved improvements which can be carried out before the body is assembled, specifically the addition of separate door and grab handles, particularly prevalent on vans, which whilst a tedious operation is well worth the results. These are easily made from fine brass wire, bent to shape. If there are to be several hand-rails of a particular size or shape, either on the same vehicle or if you are making a rake of similar vehicles, the construction of a simple jig to bend the wire to form the hand-rails is well worthwhile. For some coaches there are now etched grab-rails and door handles available, and in certain types of vehicle it may be possible to make use of these, and ease the tedium! Hand-rails, door handles, etc can easily be inserted into pre-drilled holes and 'superglued' into place. Most plastic kits provide such details ready moulded, and these can easily be removed by the careful use of a sharp, chisel-type knife blade as shown in Figure 30.

The construction of the bodywork of plastic wagon kits calls for little further comment at this stage, except for open wagons of the wooden plank type. Before the body is assembled, planking can be represented on the inside, where not moulded in, by simply scoring the plank lines on the plastic sides, ends and floor. It does improve the appearance quite considerably and takes little effort. The fitting of windows is best achieved by building a simple frame from plasticard in which to slide the glazing material. Figure 31 shows this technique.

Van roofs in both plastic and metal kits are often just a piece of thin plasticard which must be formed to shape. The best method of achieving this is shown in Figure 32.

If the resultant model is to run well, great care is needed in assembling the plastic underframes to ensure that they are square and true. Axle-boxes must be in line with each other, and the chassis should be assembled on a flat surface such as a piece of plate glass, to ensure that it will sit squarely on the track when completed. Brass bearings are fitted into pre-formed holes in the insides of the axle-boxes, and the pin-point axle ends run in these bearings and give the essential free running of the wheels. The bearings can be fixed into place in the axle-boxes with a touch of 'superglue'. Holes may need to be opened out to ensure that the bearings are seated fully home — this is

---

Figure 32 Van roofs

Roofs are often supplied as thin plastic sheet. Make a frame using van ends as templates for plasticard cross-pieces which, together with longitudinal pieces, form a good frame. Carefully made, the frame will provide an accurate location for the roof.

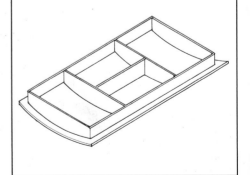

Above *A completed and painted 0–6–0 constructed from etched components.*

Right *Details such as the oil-cans and grease guns add essential character to the front end of the locomotive's etched metal tender.*

Above *This view of an AIX illustrates the level of detail essential to capture the appearance of even the humblest of locomotives.*

Below *A white metal brake-van kit, painted, lettered and ready for the road. The very lightest weathering gives an almost newly painted look, but only matt colours have been used.*

Above *The locomotive and brake van shown opposite at work on the layout. The attention to fine detail, enhanced by outdoor photography, turns kit models into a perfect re-creation of a once familar railway scene.*

Below *Another locomotive on the same layout. The milk churns, sheep, foliage and other details complete an amazingly realistic scene.*

Above *Models, or the real thing? In this photograph of the author's 'Dallington Road' layout, it's hard to tell.*

easily achieved with a small drill ($^1_{16}$ in) and a pin chuck. Ensure that when the brake gear is assembled, it is in line with the wheels and does not foul them.

More recent plastic kits may well incorporate separate mouldings of axle-box, spring and W-irons to enable wagons to be compensated. Compensation of four wheeled wagons is easily achieved, improves track holding and removes the unrealistic sight of vehicles jerking over uneven rail joints and 'nose-diving' into crossing vees on pointwork. Figure 33 shows the basic principles of compensating good stock. Most etched kits contain compensation on this principle which is designed into them with the necessary components supplied.

Compensation units can be bought separately and it is a simple matter to convert those kits which do not have compensation incorporated; the principles are shown in Figure 34. Though compensation or equalization units are available for coach bogies, I have not found them necessary for normal use, even in EM and S4.

Figure 33 Principles of wagon compensation

'W' irons are fixed to the underside of the floor. One (shown left) is rigid, the other rocks on a plate which is fastened to the wagon floor.

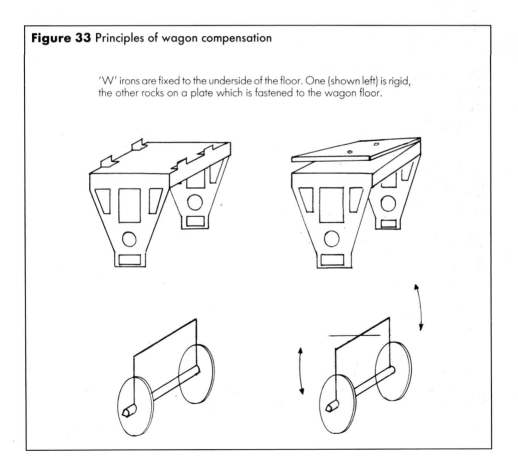

Figure 34 Compensating a rigid wagon chassis

Detailed plastic kits may provide representation of underframe beams, and these will need removing to allow etched compensation units to be fitted

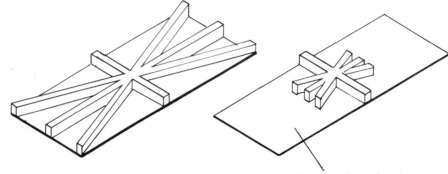

Areas at either end can be removed with a razor-saw. Floor will require sanding flat and wet-and-dry paper.

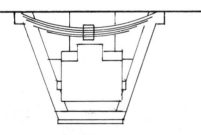

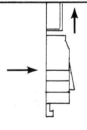

Moulded 'W'-iron, spring and axle-boxes will require removal with a razor-saw. The spring and axle-boxes are removed from the rest of the detail and retained for use on the etched 'W'-irons.

Salvaged spring is fixed to the underside of the wagon solebar, the axle-box drilled out to accept the wheel bearing and fixed over this on the outside of the 'W'-iron.

White metal kits

White metal kits are available for wagons in 4mm and 7mm scales principally from ABS. The detail in these kits is quite exemplary as is the quality of the castings and their accuracy. They follow closely the type of construction encountered in plastic kits, except that being of white metal, they require different approaches to cleaning and preparation, and to the method of fixing the parts together.

Invariably, however good the castings, some moulding flash or join lines will appear. These are easily removed using an old craft knife as a scraper, files, or wet-and-dry paper, and finishing with a burnishing tool. A 'dry run' assembly is essential to check the fit of the parts, and to ensure that you know where the parts locate and to enable you to identify any possible snags which may arise. Familiarize yourself fully with the parts and the assembly instructions, paying particular attention to any variations between different batches of basically similar types of vehicle. For example, in the SR brake-van illustrated, there are variations catered for in the kit covering the location of guards lookout duckets, vacuum cylinders and roof rainstrips. These so-called standard vehicles were rebuilt in batches from 1929 to 1948, so it is essential at an early stage to make your mind up as to which vehicle you are going to build and stick to it. Photographs can be a help in deciding detail, but photographs of wagons, particularly early period ones, are not that easy to find. There are, however, a number of excellent books on the subject of goods wagons listed in Appendix I covering a wide variety of periods and companies which will enable accurate models to be built.

When checking the fit of parts, ensure that assembly will be accurate by opening out locating holes and sockets, cleaning chamfered edges for corner joints, trimming locating pips and

The detail shown on the casting in this view of the two main assemblies of an ABS white metal brake van kit is typical of the best white metal kits. There is some detail still to be added to both body and chassis in this view of a kit under construction.

protrusions and, above all, cleaning flash from parts so that they sit neatly and accurately in their correct positions.

Assembly can be achieved by the use of low melting point solder or one of the modern 'superglues'. Soldering white metal kit components has already been covered in detail earlier in this book. Suffice it to state here that with 4mm scale white metal wagon kits, I solder the main body components together and fix the small detailed parts with 'superglue'. It is worthwhile stressing again that cleanliness is essential if these glues are to function properly. The parts to be glued should be thoroughly cleaned and the glue used very sparingly; I apply small quantities on a pin. The glue permeates well into the space between the parts to be joined and it is therefore not necessary to coat the parts to be bonded prior to holding them together — very useful when adding small detail parts. In 7mm scale, all but the smallest parts are soldered. Gluing all parts in both scales

would be equally effective and a two-part, quick-set epoxy resin would also be a suitable adhesive. Van roofs are dealt with as previously shown in Figure 32.

Before moving on to etched brass wagons and considering coaches in more detail, it is worth referring to the simple plastic N gauge wagon kits available from Peco, illustrated here. These kits are very neat, simple to assemble and provide a most realistic vehicle. They do, however, require painting, a simple enough task for BR and pre-nationalization stock, and with some of the recently introduced transfers from Woodhead models, many possibilities exist for private owner wagons too. At this point it is worth noting that painting will be simplified if the body and chassis are left separate until after painting has been completed.

Etched brass kits

Etched brass is now a common medium for wagon and coach kits and requires a

The simple components of a Peco N gauge wagon clip together and make a neat, well detailed model at a fraction of the price of the ready-finished equivalent. Note the steel bar which fits in a recess between the underframe and body to add weight to the model.

Typical components of an etched brass wagon kit, in this case an LSWR horsebox, needing only wheels, couplings, paint and transfers to complete.

totally different approach from the plastic and cast metal kits so far considered. Firstly, the components are likely to be supplied in an etched fret, such as the one shown in the illustration which is fairly typical, and these etchings will be supplemented with castings for axle-boxes, springs, dynamos, etc. The components will require removal from their frets and bending and forming into a wagon body and underframe.

The etched parts should be removed carefully from the fret by means of a chisel-type craft knife or an old knife blade. On no account should the parts be twisted from the surrounding fret or they may well be damaged and distorted. The remnants of these tabs should be carefully and neatly smoothed away with a small file and/or wet-and-dry paper to facilitate their correct and accurate fit later.

Those components that need bending to form an angle, as well as locating tabs, will usually have the bend line half

Figure 35 Bending etched components

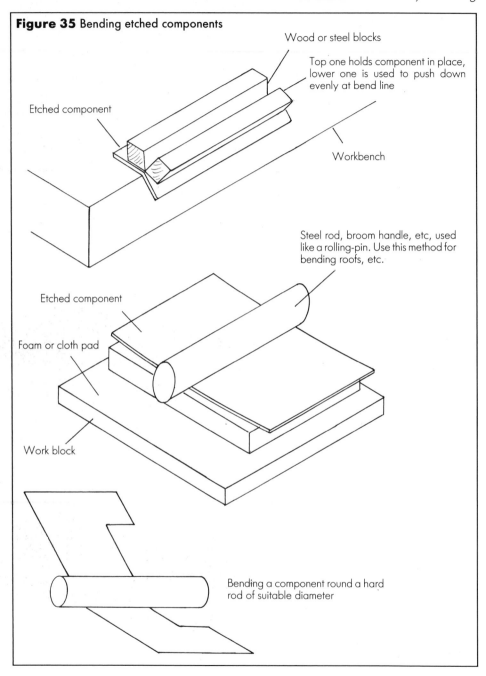

Wood or steel blocks

Top one holds component in place, lower one is used to push down evenly at bend line

Etched component

Workbench

Steel rod, broom handle, etc, used like a rolling-pin. Use this method for bending roofs, etc.

Etched component

Foam or cloth pad

Work block

Bending a component round a hard rod of suitable diameter

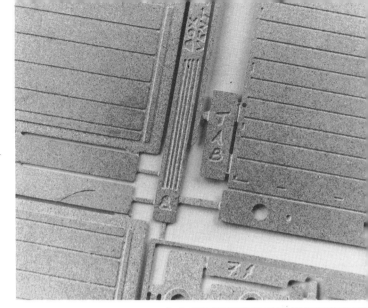

Right *Etched kits usually involve folding parts along half-etched lines, with the half-etched line usually on the inside. In the example shown here, though, the line on the tab is on the outside of the fold.*

Right *The basic underframe solebars folded up and step boards folded out. The brake handle, V-hangers and links are soldered and the cast vacuum cylinder soldered into place.*

Right *Cast axleguards and springs are fixed inside the solebar.*

The basic body shell assembled with the vents soldered inside the openings.

etched, and this should normally be on the inside of any fold. Components can be bent quite simply and evenly with a little improvisation and the use of scrap timber. Some ideas for this are shown in Figure 35. The most difficult item to fold neatly from flat is the solebar channel section. Here, patience, a good vice and the use of steel or hardwood longer than the piece to be formed are the main aids.

It is possible to assemble some etched brass kits with 'superglue', such as those which are of tab-and-slot assembly, but I always solder them. Ordinary tinman's solder or multicore solder will be ideal for the main parts, with low-melt solder used to fix castings and some detail parts. The illustrations show the principle stages in the assembly of an etched brass wagon.

It is quite common for the builder to have to supply his own floor in an etched kit. This is easily done using,

say, 40 thou plasticard for O gauge and thinner material for 4mm scale. Usually this floor will locate on etched stretchers between the vehicle sides or on the solebar. This floor should obviously be square and accurately fitted, and often provides the location for detailed parts such as vacuum brake cylinders. It may even provide the base for compensation units. Your floor therefore needs to be strong and rigid enough for this purpose.

There are vehicles which require overlaps of panelling or outside frames to be fitted to the main body sides. If possible, and this will depend on the design of the kit, it is easier to fix this whilst the main parts are flat. Clearly, where a tumble-home or other shaping is needed, then the parts should be pre-formed before being soldered together. My method of sweating these details on is shown in Figure 36. The pins holding the sides down flat are also

Figure 36 Fixing panelling overlays

Sweat main components together

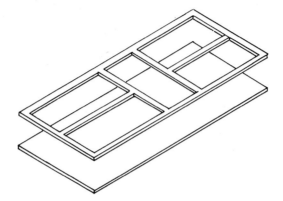

Tin final overlay with a lower
melting point solder if available.
Hold in place with pins and apply
the hot iron, moving steadily along
in one direction. Do not allow the
iron to dwell too long on one spot
and buckle the assembly — just
long enough to fuse the solder.

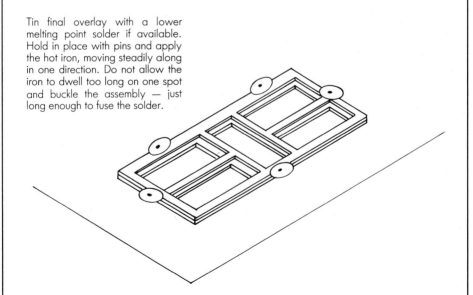

an aid to accurate location which may be further helped by the judicious use of dressmakers' pins. The surfaces which will be joined are tinned and fluxed, and, when accurately located, the hot iron is applied. I work quickly and evenly along the joint and using this method have had little or no trouble with distortion, providing that a sufficiently hot iron is used and that it is not left to dwell too long at any one point. Any minor distortion which occurs is easily manipulated away with the fingers or smoothed out on a flat surface.

Provided that such parts are scrupulously cleaned, it is possible to 'superglue' overlays to the main body panels, but if you are going to solder in the vicinity of any parts so assembled at a later stage, beware, because the heat will destroy the bond of 'superglue'. Murphy's law will always mean that the bit which doesn't stick or becomes unbonded will be at the most noticeable, crucial or inaccessible point! It is better therefore to ensure that the whole lot is properly fixed at the outset and left well alone, hence the use of soldering.

Where separate corner-plates, strapping, door-plates, locks and hinges are intended to be located flat on to the body, I use 'superglue' for all but the largest parts, but leave this operation until last, in fact until after the model has been cleaned but immediately before painting. Where the roofs provided are merely a rectangle of plastic card, this should be carefully trimmed to size, ensuring the correct overhang and taking care that it is cut squarely. Figure 32 shows how this can be done. Add rainstrips from plasticard microstrip and ventilators from castings, which are usually provided with the kit.

There is little else to say on the construction of goods vehicles, other than to consider some of the alterations and improvements which can be made to kits. The addition of compensation has been covered, and it has been assumed that the builder would have discarded any plastic wheels included with the kit and substituted them with steel-tyred wheels and pin-point bearings. Such wheels and bearings are readily available from Alan Gibson and Maygib in 4mm scale and Slaters and Alan Gibson in 7mm scale. The use of such wheels and bearings not only improves the appearance but also provides superior free running in a squarely and accurately assembled chassis.

Those kits of open wagons which do not provide interior planking for the sides and ends can have the plank join lines scribed very simply with a steel straight edge and knife, with the point of the knife blade held at 90° to the steel ruler. This improvement should be made before assembly. If you intend to place a load in an open wagon, then you may be happy to score the top one or two plank lines only. Remember that the lines should match those moulded on the outside.

Goods wagons lasted very many years and even well into the 1950s the majority of open wagons were of the wooden-bodied type, often former private owner wagons. They took quite a battering in use and, particularly in later years, could often be seen with the quite obvious results of repair and improvement. It is quite easy to add some individuality to 'standard' wagons built from kits, and very many wagon conversions, such as the Airfix (now Dapol) BR mineral wagon, have been described in the model railway press, as listed in the Appendix. A much easier way of achieving individuality is to represent some of the repairs and modifications on your models, for example the replacement of a buffer with one of a different type, the fitting in early vehicles of brakes on one side only, or the substitution of the brake gear provided with the kit with a different type (detailed wagon brake castings are readily available from ABS and Kenline). Standard wagons can also be made to represent engineers' department stock, finished in appropriate departmental stock livery, with simple improvements such as the addition of

tarpaulin covers over the axle-boxes of open wagons used for ballast trains. Reference to books and photographs will reveal many simple changes which can be made to add individuality with little effort.

Before the last war, the vast majority of general merchandise was carried in open wagons, sheeted over with tarpaulins. This situation prevailed until the late 1950s and is easily represented in model form as shown in Figure 37. Another easy variation which could be seen occasionally is a mix of wheel types, say one axle with split spoke wheels and the other with ordinary spokes suggesting replacement during some repair.

Figure 37 Wagon tarpaulins

Fold up a cover or 'lid' from foil and paint grey/black and letter as appropriate

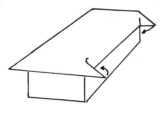

'Sag' the centre and add a spot of varnish to represent a puddle. In larger scales add ropes from cotton.

CHAPTER 8
Painting goods stock

The painting and finishing of goods stock is an easy enough task. Preparation of the surfaces, removal of any burrs and flash and the filling of gaps with Milliput or similar is very important, and time will be well spent ensuring a good surface to take the paint. Livery details should be established before the painting is commenced. I spray-paint wagon underframes using car touch-up aerosol. If possible, split the body from the chassis for painting, but do not worry if this is not possible as it is a simple matter to mask the wagon body with paper and masking tape whilst painting the chassis.

It is essential to remove any traces of flux and excess solder from the metal kits before painting, and use of a fibreglass burnishing tool will help to ensure a smooth, even surface and remove any surplus glue or solder. Use sight and feel to establish the finish and, when you are happy with it, an application of lighter fuel on a cotton pad will clean off any final traces of grease. Be careful with this fluid as it is highly flammable, and its fumes are dangerous if inhaled in a confined space for any length of time.

Prime any metal kits with car aerosol touch-up paint primer before painting the top coat. When this has thoroughly dried it will show up any imperfections which could not be seen beforehand, and these should be treated and a further coat of primer applied before the top coat. These car aerosol paints are very useful, and the primers give a nice matt mid grey or bauxite colour to wagon bodies. The gloss paints in the touch-up aerosols are so vast in their range of colour and shade that often the colour you need for a model is available. They are useful for locomotives, as already discussed, coaches, vans and passenger-rated vehicles such as horseboxes, which often had a finish to match their contemporary coaching stock.

These paints require the application of several light coats, allowing a good hour between coats to build up a finish. Being cellulose based, they dry quickly to a vary hard surface, and after a few days lining or further detailed painting can be carried out with enamel paints. If a mistake is made, the enamel can easily be removed without damaging the cellulose surface of the main body colour below.

For wagon bodies in 4mm scale (except passenger-rated vehicles finished similarly to coaches) and 7mm scale open wagons, I brush paint. The secret is to use a good quality brush, much larger than you would think appropriate, size 4 for 4mm, size 7 for 7mm, and apply new paint, thinned and *well-stirred*, taking two or sometimes three coats. I always use matt paints for wagons as a wagon with a high gloss surface just does not look right on a model, except for vehicles finished in passenger liveries. Allow overnight drying between coats, placing the model in a spacious, clean box to protect it from dust which will affect the finish. Air brushing, if you have one, is obviously a most acceptable way of finishing wagons and particularly useful if a batch of vehicles is to be painted at one time.

If individuality can be added easily by modifying, adding or leaving out parts, then it can just as easily be added with paint. As already noted, goods wagons worked hard for their living and even in the golden age of railways before the First World War, when locos and coaches were immaculately turned out, wagons were not subject to the rigours of cleaners.

Weathering and dirtying of locomotives and stock is a much debated topic amongst railway modellers in Great Britain, but it is already the normal practice in the USA, where standards of realism achieved are quite fantastic. It is my view that, particularly with goods stock, a weathered finish on most vehicles is an integral part of creating stock on a working layout and should be carried out.

The basic technique involved in weathering wagons, or making them look used, is observation. Take a look at the real thing if you can, especially if you model the contemporary scene. Some good ideas can be found from photographs in specialized wagon books for ealier periods. At its most basic, the process may simply be the representation of lime wash seeping and splashing through cattle wagon sides from the inside out. At its most complex, it is an artistic masterpiece where every aspect is covered, down to the splits and indentations in woodwork.

Conveniently, if rather simplistically, weathering can be categorized as follows:

1 The overall film of dirt any object gets when left outside, and weather fading.
2 The dirt and stains caused by the use of the vehicle; for example, coal dust or sand.
3 Rust on exposed metal, such as running gear, bolt heads, etc.
4 Deposits from brake fittings around the underframe.
5 Special details such as the aforementioned lime wash stains on cattle wagons, spillage around tank fillers on oil tank wagons, or grease marks around axle-boxes and other moving parts such as brake lever pivots.

This list also represents a convenient order for the processes, which you can carry out to whatever degree you consider appropriate. Remember that wagons do not weather equally, so each one should be treated to varying degrees.

The first step is to paint and finish, the wagon including any lettering, as if it were new. When this is dry, the overall grime colour is applied. Here an air brush, whilst useful, is not as essential; a large, good quality brush and a wash of well-stirred and thinned matt paint will do. The choice of colour is, obviously, down to your own preference and observation. I use a dark, dirty brown-grey from the Humbrol range, No 66, and vary its shade slightly by the addition of a little matt white or matt black to lighten or darken it; I also use a varied consistency for the wash, adding more or less thinner to particular vehicles. The greater the number of washes, the greater the colour density achieved.

The second stage is the addition of the discoloration of use. Clearly, the colour used here will depend on the load the vehicle carries, for example black for coal, milk/off-white for china clay, etc. Study of pictures of the vehicles concerned will give an indication of where this weathering should be applied. There are plenty of photographs in specialist books which show up easily the effect on, for example, china clay wagons. Black coal dust is not as easily discernible in black and white photographs, but Jane's colour albums provide a good reference source.

A different technique is called for in applying the paint at this stage, and that is dry brushing. Dry brushing is a simple technique whereby a brush loaded with an appropriate colour has most of the paint wiped from it; it will, however, retain some remnants of paint which could only be removed by washing in thinners, and it is these remnants which are required on the model. Rubbing the now nearly empty brush across the chosen part of the model will leave the paint in uneven streaks, particularly on raised detail. With practice, a considerable and use-

ful variety of finishes can be achieved with dry brushing, the continued use of which can build up the finish to the level you require. A similar process is stippling the surface with the brush (a round stencil brush is ideal), and this is an effective way of providing particular effects such as rust on a steel-bodied mineral wagon.

The third stage, adding rust to steelwork, can be achieved with a combination of a wash and dry brushing. For a wagon newly returned to service after a repaint, the brake gear and rigging can be given a light wash of rust colour. Similarly, a slight dry brushing of rust on the body ironwork, such as the bolt heads and strapping and hinges, can be very effective in helping to depict a well-used wagon. Be careful not to overdo it as, with all weathering, subtlety is the key to success.

The fourth stage is to add track colour, dry brushed again (only a little is needed) around the brake-shoes. Small amounts of gloss black around the axle-boxes can hint at old grease and oil deposits.

Lastly comes the addition of speciality weathering such as the previously mentioned lime wash to cattle wagons, and oil spillage around the filler caps of oil tank wagons. The former is represented by liberally splashing the interior, particularly the floor and lower body sides, with a matt off-white, which is allowed to spill out to the outside of the lower body, and over the underframe. If you cannot get into the body for this, dry brush a similar colour on the outside. This will probably be necessary anyway to supplement the first method and to get anything but a very light coating. Gloss black is carefully applied around and streaked down the sides of oil tanks to represent spillage from filling.

Two further touches of individuality can be added. It was common practice to patch and repair wooden-bodied wagons and, particularly in the postwar period, for the replacement planking not to be painted. Individual planks can be picked out in a pale grey/buff colour to represent this.

Steel-bodied mineral vehicles, such as the ubiquitous BR 16-ton wagons, are often seen very heavily rusted, and, if you want an authentic-looking train composed of these vehicles, then typically this would range from an odd one very clean almost new looking, through various stages of rusting and toning down of paintwork by the weather, to an odd one that is almost totally rust covered. This is easily achieved by a combination of dry brushing and stippling of the body with rust paint, the shade of which is changed repeatedly, but subtly, by adding track colour and/or matt black. For some reason, even in badly rusted bodies, the white diagonal stripe indicating the end door seems to survive pretty well intact, but in badly rusted wagons takes on an orange-coloured staining.

It is possible to achieve the crazed, flaking effect of the rust by using cellulose paint to weather on top of enamel base coats, but great care is needed to avoid damage to a plastic body. Dry brushing matt black into the rust, but sparingly, will indicate coal dust which has been deposited. Some colour illustrations of wagons weathered as described are included.

CHAPTER 9
Coaches

Plastic kits

The basics of plastic coach body construction are similar to those for wagons discussed above, and, if the following notes are read together with the text on wagon body construction, there is little further to concern the builder of plastic coach kits save painting and lining and the provision of interiors which will be dealt with later. The underframe does, however, warrant some consideration.

The bogies must be assembled accurately and squarely and, for better running, plastic wheels, if supplied, should be substituted by steel-tyred wheels running on pin-point axles in brass bearings, fitted as described for wagon underframes. Assembly should be on a true, flat surface — a piece of glass for preference — and with the axle-boxes exactly facing each other. Liquid polystyrene cement is sufficient for assembly, and the bogies should be put on one side and allowed to set thoroughly before assembly to the body.

The detail parts on plastic coach kits are very fine and it will be found easier to clean any moulding flash from them as far as possible whilst they are still on their sprues, leaving only the remnants of the sprue join to be cleaned off after their removal.

It is worth considering applying the more complex liveries, with fully lined-out panelling on the sides, before the coach is assembled. Clearly a dry run is necessary to ensure that the main body parts fit accurately, and any holes drilled to avoid subsequent damage to the paintwork. The sides can then be painted and allowed to dry thoroughly before lining and lettering are carried out (see Chapter 10).

There is one type of plastic body kit, prevalent in O gauge, which is worthy of special consideration. This type of kit comprises of vacuum-formed plastic sides, ends and roof and the builder is left to provide his own underframe, bogies, buffers, etc. They are a comparatively cheap means of building O

Right *The fineness of detail can clearly be seen in this view of the components of a plastic coach kit. Parts, particularly on the underframe and bogie sprues, are arranged closely together and great care is needed in cutting these free. The plastic wheeels provided should be discarded for steel-tyred wheels running in brass bearings.*

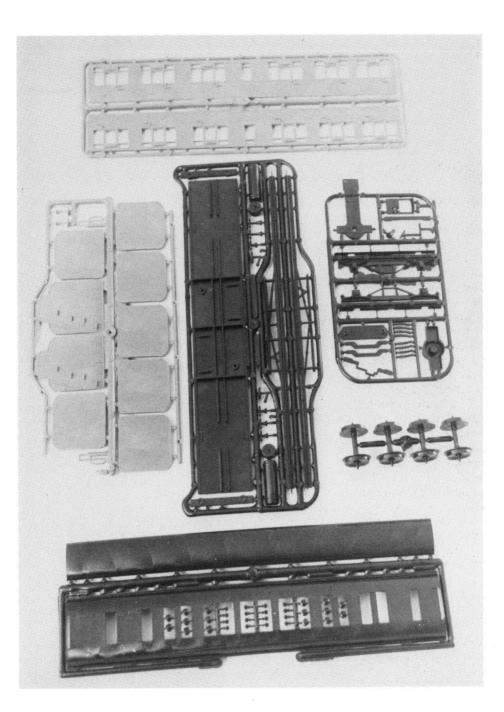

Left *Plastic bogie side-frames, with a brass bearing inserted, and the pin-point axle which it will carry.*

Left *A completed plastic bogie.*

Below *The major sub-assemblies of the plastic coach kit. The assemblies are separate, to ease painting, detailing and particularly lining.*

Figure 38 Construction of vacuum-formed plastic kits

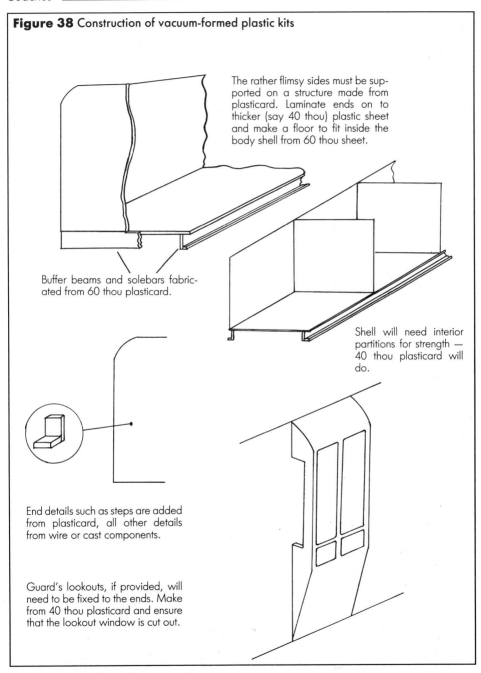

The rather flimsy sides must be supported on a structure made from plasticard. Laminate ends on to thicker (say 40 thou) plastic sheet and make a floor to fit inside the body shell from 60 thou sheet.

Buffer beams and solebars fabricated from 60 thou plasticard.

Shell will need interior partitions for strength — 40 thou plasticard will do.

End details such as steps are added from plasticard, all other details from wire or cast components.

Guard's lookouts, if provided, will need to be fixed to the ends. Make from 40 thou plasticard and ensure that the lookout window is cut out.

gauge coaching stock and provide a most acceptable model. They do, however, require a fair bit of work on the part of the builder. The body will need support and strengthening from internal partitions, a false roof and, of course, the floor. This can all be achieved easily using plasticard, and the general principle is shown in Figure 38. Door handles and grab-rails are

---

Figure 39 Forming wire hand-rails and door handles

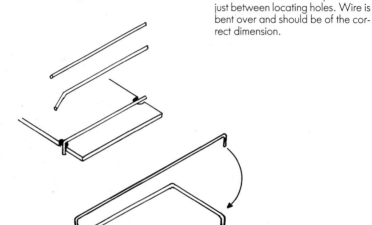

Plasticard or similar scrap cut to fit just between locating holes. Wire is bent over and should be of the correct dimension.

Grab-rails and angled hand-rails are best bent after the short lengths at the end have been formed, but this calls for careful calculation. A jig can be used to speed up production and aid accuracy if several similar ones are needed.

Handles are easily formed by filing small pins — track pins are ideal in the smaller scales

easily added from brass wire or etchings, as shown in Figure 39.

The construction of the underframe using plasticard, or building one up from brass angle, is quite straightforward. Underframes do, of course, vary significantly from vehicle to vehicle and reference to books and articles on coaching stock and, where available, drawings, is essential to get the detail correct. There are many types of fittings such as buffers, dynamos, battery boxes, queen-posts for truss-rods, etc available as castings or turnings, which cover most requirements. High quality cast metal bogies are available from Cavalier Coaches.

Metal kits

Metal coach kits are of basically two types. The first has an aluminium body shell either made up from separate sides, roof and ends, or a pre-formed body and roof shell requiring only the addition of cast ends to make a basic body (this latter type is more common in 7mm scale). The next section deals with this type. Secondly is the etched brass type which has a variety of different constructional designs.

The essential requirement is as always for a square, accurate assembly of the sides and ends, which is where assembly starts. The cast ends must be fastened to the sides with epoxy resin adhesive — the quick-setting type will do. It is essential that the surfaces that are to be bonded are clean, and a quick rub with a fibreglass burnishing tool will achieve this. Ensure that there are no burrs on the ends of the sides, removing any which may be found with a small file and finishing smooth with wet-and-dry paper. Similarly, ensure that there is nothing on the cast

Plastic is an ideal medium for fully panelled coaches; but plastic coach kits are also available for more modern vehicles such as the Maunsell coaches shown here. The two locomotives are built from white metal kits.

ends to prevent a good fit against the side. Remove any restrictive lumps or moulding flash with a craft knife and files. When you are happy with the fit, the parts can be glued together. Only a thin film is required as too much glue will not allow the parts to fit together properly. Hold the assembly together with rubber bands and ensure that it is square before putting it on one side to set thoroughly. Any epoxy which squeezes out from the joints should be wiped away before it sets.

Some cast coach ends contain cast-on details such as pipework, lighting conduits and even hand-rails, but these are worth replacing with separate ones bent up from wire. If you decide to undertake this improvement, it will be necessary to do so before assembling the body shell. The cast-on detail can be removed with a *sharp*, heavy-duty knife, paring and scraping away a little at a time. A file can then be used, finishing the surface with wet-and-dry paper and finally the burnishing tool. Some ideas for these improvements are shown in Figure 40.

It is convenient to pursue work on the underframe whilst the body shell is allowed to set. The underframe will locate on the cast-in ledge on the coach ends, and it is useful to arrange for it to be removable to gain access to the interior. This can often be achieved by the use of small self-tapping screws through the floor into the ledges.

There are a few points to watch in building up the underframes. The bogie mountings should be central and at the correct distance for the type of underframe modelled. The truss-rods will, in 4mm scale, usually be plastic mouldings. Ensure that they are correctly positioned and central to the vehicle, otherwise they may foul the bogie and prevent it from pivoting. The usual arrangement for mounting the bogies is for the mounts to hold captive a nut or bolt. A securing screw or nut then holds the bogie in place. It is quite possible that the bogie will need spacing to allow the coach to sit at the correct buffer height. This is best achieved with the addition of a washer which should ideally be near enough the diameter of the mounting or slightly larger to prevent the vehicle rocking too much. The washer (or washers, as more

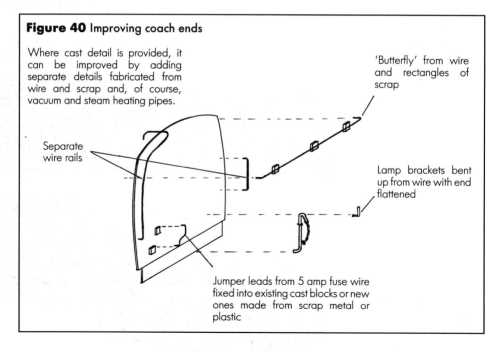

Figure 40 Improving coach ends

Where cast detail is provided, it can be improved by adding separate details fabricated from wire and scrap and, of course, vacuum and steam heating pipes.

'Butterfly' from wire and rectangles of scrap

Separate wire rails

Lamp brackets bent up from wire with end flattened

Jumper leads from 5 amp fuse wire fixed into existing cast blocks or new ones made from scrap metal or plastic

Cast metal O gauge bogies and underframe parts.

The bogie mounting block with washers to bring the coach to the correct height, as described.

This detailed underframe comprises castings, etched brass and wire, all on a wooden floor.

The basic underframe constructed from plasticard and detailed with readily available castings is not difficult to build and makes a very effective O gauge vehicle from comparatively cheap plastic body shell parts.

than one may exceptionally be required) goes between the mount and the bogie, as illustrated.

Castings or mouldings will provide the rest of the underframe detail such as battery boxes, dynamos, vacuum cylinders, etc, and these can be epoxied or 'superglued' to the underside of the floor. Add footboards to the solebars as necessary from strips of plasticard 'superglued' in place.

At this stage I normally paint the underframes with a coat of primer (car aerosol touch-up primer) and a light coat or two of matt black from the same source. The underframe can then be put on one side to allow the paint to harden off.

The bogies, which are invariably, both in 4mm and 7mm scales, cast metal with this type of kit, require a little comment. Assembly should, of course, be square and true, and the bogie built up on a flat surface such as a piece of plate glass. Steel-tyred wheels and brass pin-point bearings are essential, the bearings being held in place with a touch of 'superglue'. It may be necessary to open out the holes in the cast bogie sideframes to enable the bearings to be located properly, and a suitable drill in a pin chuck will do the job nicely.

Assembly of these bogies usually involves cast sideframes with axle-box and spring detail incorporated, a central stretcher with provision for mounting, and two end pieces, together with additional detailing such as brakes. The main components can be glued or soldered together with low-melt solder as described on page 16. I favour soldering this assembly, and fixing fine details with 'superglue'. It can be a bit fiddly holding the wheels in

place whilst fixing the bogie together, but perseverance rather than any patent method provides the answer. Whether you use fingers or rubber bands, remember to ensure that the assembly is flat down on the glass when fixing to achieve a square, true assembly, otherwise running will be impaired. I then spray the bogies with the matt black aerosol, wheels as well, and put these on one side to dry off while work on the body resumes.

Droplights at doorways will need to be added to the body shell from the inside, and, if not provided, can easily be cut from thin plasticard and fixed to the inside wall. Some drop lights can, if you wish, be fixed in the 'open' position. Figure 41 shows how these can be cut.

Attention can now be turned to detailing the roof, and, if it is a separate extrusion, fixing it in place. If the roof is not pre-drilled, a plan showing where lamp tops, ventilators, etc are located is normally included. Take care that the correct layout is chosen for the vehicle you are building and that where detail is 'handed', as it were, such as the fixing of ventilators over compartments, not on the corridor side, that the roof is fixed on the right way round! Roof details are usually cast and those such as ventilators locate in holes in the roof. Drilling these is a simple task with a suitable sized drill. A small electric 12 volt mini-drill is definitely a boon here, as well as in drilling holes in the sides to locate hand-rails, grab-rails, door handles, etc, which can easily be fabricated from wire and track pins respectively as shown in Figure 39, and fixed in place with glue. Make sure that these fixings do not protrude much into the inside as they will hinder the fixing of glazing later.

Figure 41 Droplights

Droplights are fixed inside the door
and may be fixed closed or half
open as shown.

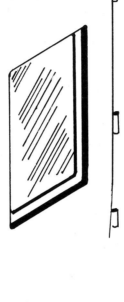

Drop lights are easily made from 10 or 20 thou plasticard

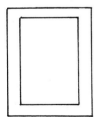

Cut out the basic rectangle
slightly larger than the window
opening in the vehicle side.
Mark the inner rectangle which
is to be removed.

With a sharp craft knife, remove
the centre but cut the corners at
an angle.

Angled corners are rounded
with a needle file.

Plastic coach seating is readily available for 4mm and 7mm scales and forms the basis of detailed interiors.

Detail is added to the ends as shown in Figure 40, and corridor connections, where appropriate, buffers, couplings and any vacuum or train heating pipes added.

The body shell can now be cleaned up, any surplus glue removed, joints at the ends smoothed and filled and attention given to the interior.

My preference is to build the interior directly on to the floor of the underframe. The basic material is plasticard, using seat moulding which is available for both 4mm and 7mm scales. Figure 42 shows clearly the basic construction. The level of detail subsequently

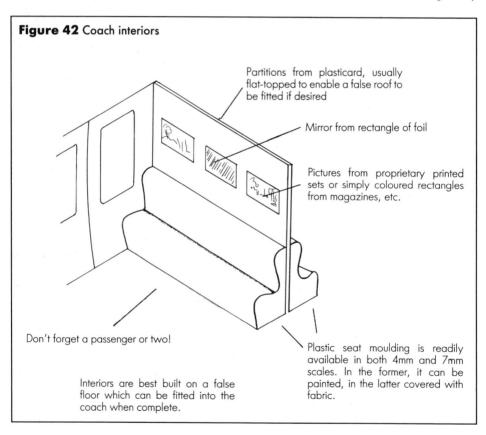

Figure 42 Coach interiors

Partitions from plasticard, usually flat-topped to enable a false roof to be fitted if desired

Mirror from rectangle of foil

Pictures from proprietary printed sets or simply coloured rectangles from magazines, etc.

Don't forget a passenger or two!

Interiors are best built on a false floor which can be fitted into the coach when complete.

Plastic seat moulding is readily available in both 4mm and 7mm scales. In the former, it can be painted, in the latter covered with fabric.

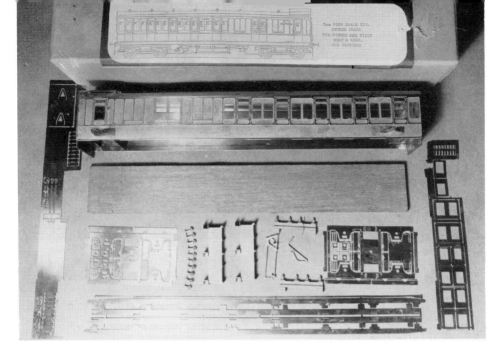

Components of an etched brass coach kit. In this example, the body shell is pre-formed with integral sides and roof. Construction has already begun, with the ends and birdcage roof added. In addition to the parts shown, numerous castings are supplied for detailing, and for parts such as springs, axle-boxes and buffers.

added by the builder is left to personal choice and is, I think, largely governed by scale. The very least that I believe should be portrayed is seating, compartment partitions and corridor walls. In 7mm scale it is worth adding representations of pictures, mirrors, seat arms and, not least, people. It is quite possible even in 4mm scale to provide very detailed interiors should this take your fancy.

Last but not least comes the painting, lining and lettering of the coach body which is dealt with in Chapter 10.

Etched brass kits

The second type of metal coach kit is made from etched brass, and a fairly typical set of components is illustrated. The body shells, like those of the aluminium ones, are designed for assembly

in different ways. Some are ready formed into roof and sides, others fold up into floor and sides with the roof as a separate piece, and some comprise separate sides, ends, floor and roof.

The parts will require careful removal from the fret as described for etched wagons. The basic construction usually involves folding parts from flat into a box for the body shell, adding sections for solebars and bending parts at 90° to form V supports for brake linkage and rods. The principles for assemblies of this nature follow those outlined in the earlier section on etched wagon kits. Additionally, however, it will be necessary not only to solder the ends between the body sides, but also partitions or body stretchers, and the body must be kept square.

Partitions are usually contained on

Above *Etched coach kits usually include cross-pieces which serve two purposes — to mount the bogies and connect the sides together. A plasticard floor will be added.*

Below *The basic assembly of an etched coach body with separate sides and ends can be seen. The components are stained, but this can easily be burnished into a polished brass surface before painting.*

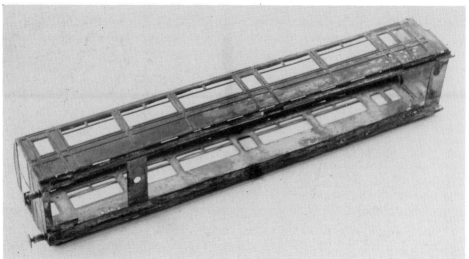

Above *An etched coach body kit with integral sides and roof to which ends and interiors are added.*

Below *Early stages in the construction of etched bogies. Folded up from flat, joints with stretchers should be soldered for strength before cast details, axle-boxes and springs are added.*

the etched fret and, after cleaning up and removing any burrs or tabs, they can be soldered inside the coach body. Where the body shell is made from separate sides and ends, squareness and general assembly can be eased with the use of blocks and jigs such as those shown in Figure 29.

Etched bogies are the norm with this type of kit, and usually the sideframes are folded at 90° to the integrally etched main stretcher. I prefer to add a fillet of solder to strengthen this key point when I am satisfied with the angle.

Cast detail (and sometimes etched brake parts) is added and the choice here is between low-melt solder and 'superglue'. I use the latter for small detail castings, but the main axle-boxes, springs, larger detail and any further brass work I solder using the same technique described for fixing castings to locomotives. The bearings for the pin-point axles go through the brass sideframe into the casting.

With etched kits, holes are usually etched in for hand-rails and other such details, but may need opening out with drill and pin chuck. The door handles and grab-rails may be provided from etchings or turnings, but hand-rails will require forming from wire. Figure 39 shows some aids to forming hand-rails.

It is quite common for end steps to be formed by bending from flat and

A basic etched bogie to which castings are added for details. The arrangement for mounting the bogie on the underside of the floor on a cast block can be seen.

Another bogie from etched components, this one with footboards.

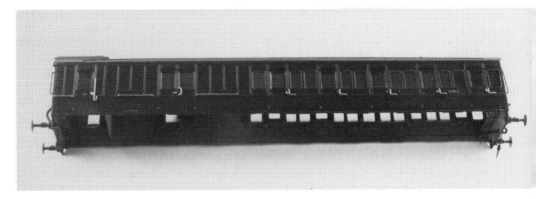

Above *A completed etched coach body.*

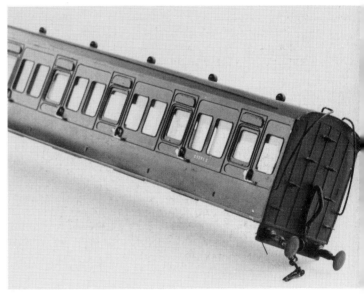

Right *The fine detail possible in etched kits is worth the effort.*

sometimes they push through slots in the outer 'skin' end pieces. It is a good idea to solder the steps and add a fillet of solder at the bend lines or where they protrude through, to give a little more strength to these delicate and vulnerable parts.

Detailing and finishing of the etched coach is much the same as that described for other metal coach kits, until it comes to the cleaning and prepa-ration. Excess solder should be removed, being careful to avoid damage to raised detail. Wet-and-dry paper finishing and a once-over with the burnishing tool is the favoured way. Large or awkward solder excess can be scraped away with a craft knife.

It is usually possible to arrange for the underframe and body to remain separate for painting and detailing the interior.

CHAPTER 10
Painting and lining coaches

Painting and lining is a straightforward operation and, whilst lining out panelling on older vehicles with fully-lined liveries is quite tricky, with patience and a little practice a satisfying result can be achieved.

The preparation of the body should provide a smooth, clean surface on which to apply the paint. Once any imperfections have been filled, smoothed and cleaned, the model can be primed. With plastic sides, I find cleaning will principally involve the removal of dust and plastic filings etc, which congregate, hidden away, only to emerge to show through the paint later! A photographer's lens-cleaning brush with its rubber bulb blower is useful for this work. With metal sides, it is a question of removing residues of glue, flux and grease. I find lighter fuel applied with a cotton pad is excellent for this. Care should be taken with the use of this liquid as it is highly flammable and its fumes are dangerous if inhaled for too long in a confined space.

Priming is the next consideration, and although special primers are available for various types of metal, I find once again that ordinary grey aerosol paint sold as an undercoat for car touch-up paints is perfectly satisfactory for all the materials considered in this section, including plastic. Light coats should be applied rather than attempting to coat the model fully in one go, and it should be touch dry before re-coating. Check that all blemishes have been eradicated — the matt grey will highlight any which could not be seen before priming — and remedy any with the careful use of fine wet-and-dry paper and/or filler as appropriate.

When you are happy with the grey primer and it has been allowed to dry, the top coat can be applied to the body. Here there is a choice between car aerosol touch-up paints, the colour range of which is so vast that invariably a fair, if not exact, match can be found, and the aerosol paints developed specially for the model maker, such as those by Humbrol or Precision. The latter range is matched to a large selection of railway colours.

It is worth noting that the colour applied to locomotives and rolling-stock causes as much controversy as any other aspect of the hobby. Irrespective of manufacturing or technical reasons for colour changes, col-

Above *The text refers to colourful painting of and advertising on plate girder bridges. A contemporary example, a rather bright and welcome relief from grey, is shown here. This 'fashion' for painting bridges of this type is becoming quite common.*

Above *An example of brickwork painted as described in the text, showing only a small section of the possible colour variations. The bare unpainted plasticard is visible at the extreme right-hand side of the picture.*

Below *Stonework painted as described in the text. As with brickwork, the colour variation possibilities are endless.*

Below *A roof with exposed timbers and a boarded-up window are very simply made by adapting plastic building kits.*

Above *An etched brass horsebox body detailed with end beading, ventilators and hinges, all sweated into place. The discoloration of the brass is inevitable during construction and will be removed when the model is burnished before painting.*

Left *The same model at a later stage of construction, after having its first coat of primer and awaiting only the addition of roof and interior which will be added after the model has been painted.*

Above *Two varying degrees of weathering applied to steel-bodied wagons and carried out as described in the text.*

Below left *A well-weathered cattle wagon showing lime wash staining as described in the text.*

Below right *A wooden-bodied wagon painted and weathered and showing some of the many effects which can be created with the paintbrush.*

Above *Careful painting and finishing adds tremendously to the finished appearance of a model. The 4mm scale vehicle on the left looks quite effective and shows that the result justifies the effort.*

Below *A well detailed farmer's float from the Dart Castings kit in its first coat of primer and awaiting the addition of reins, a driver and load.*

our is a very personal thing, and each of us may well perceive a colour in a particular and yet slightly different way, and that takes no account of colour blindness! My view is that the matched colour ranges such as that of Precision are quite accurate enough and will certainly suffice.

I think that spraying is essential to get a nice even gloss finish on coaching stock. The whole body sides are sprayed and, again several light coats building up the colour surface are better than one heavy coat. The body sides can be masked with tape when they are fully dry and the paint has had a little time to harden, and the roof and ends painted. It will be necessary on some vehicles to paint the droplights a different colour from the main body sides and this must be done with a fine brush. Where the livery has a two-tone body side, the body should be sprayed with the lighter colour first, and when this has dried it can be masked with tape and the darker colour applied.

The varnished teak livery of the LNER and some other pre-grouping companies is difficult to represent. There have been many methods detailed in the model railway press for achieving this finish with excellent results. The simplest method I have found, which is quite effective but which, I accept does not necessarily have the best finish, is to spray the body sides with cream paint and to apply with a brush a quite fluid wash of a suitable brown, tan or similar shade. The idea is to let the cream base just show in fine streaks through the brown. It may be necessary to apply more than one coat of brown.

Lining out coaches is not as difficult as it seems at first glance, particularly those simple liveries requiring only straight lines. There are some lining transfers available for certain liveries and these will either be of the water-slide or Pressfix type. The former, despite any suggestion that it is not necessary, should be trimmed right to the edge of the design, but otherwise applied as per the instructions. These transfers can be quite versatile and with care and the aid of a *sharp* scalpel — and a bit of ingenuity — they can give a fair representation of the fully panelled livery as applied for example to flush-sided stock by the LMS at one period. The basics of this technique are shown in Figure 43. Long straight lines need some care; a straight edge can be used to check that the transfer is actually straight. If you do not check and adjust at this stage, you are sure to discover that it's crooked when a coat of varnish has been applied and nothing can be done! Adjustments can be made by moistening the transfer, re-positioning it correctly and smoothing it down again. It is important to ensure that the transfer is flat down to the surface, and there are preparations available to ensure that transfers 'lie down' over, say, rivet detail.

The Pressfix-type transfers are also quite versatile and can be adapted as described above. Care is also needed to ensure that the lines are straight and the straight edge is essential. Unlike water-slide transfers, they cannot be adjusted when rubbed down fully, so care is needed to ensure the transfer is straight before it is pressed home and the backing paper removed. This type of lining is very fine and can often be used to good effect on moulded panelling, without overhanging the raised mouldings. These lining transfers are gen-

Figure 43 Adapting waterslide transfers for coach lining

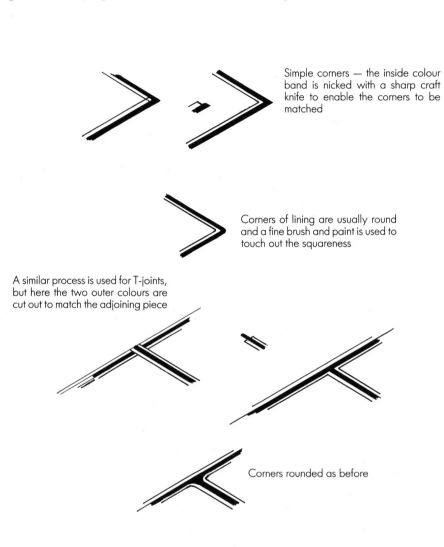

Simple corners — the inside colour band is nicked with a sharp craft knife to enable the corners to be matched

Corners of lining are usually round and a fine brush and paint is used to touch out the squareness

A similar process is used for T-joints, but here the two outer colours are cut out to match the adjoining piece

Corners rounded as before

Figure 44 Using a bow-pen

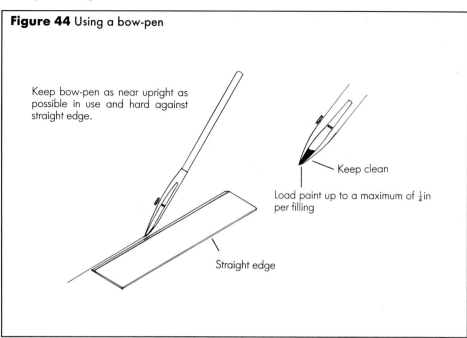

Keep bow-pen as near upright as possible in use and hard against straight edge.

Keep clean

Load paint up to a maximum of $\frac{1}{4}$ in per filling

Straight edge

Figure 45 Simple support for lining

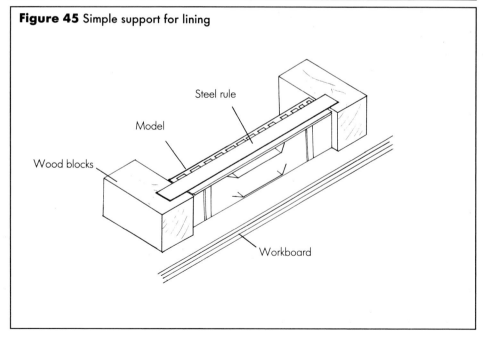

Steel rule

Model

Wood blocks

Workboard

An O gauge vehicle completed as described in the text, an effective model at a very reasonable cost, well rewards a little care and extra effort by the builder.

erally available only for 4mm scale, but I find them equally effective in 7mm scale, particularly the coarser water-slide type.

Lettering is available for all pre-nationalization and some pre-Grouping British railway companies and British Rail through to the present day. Also, vast ranges of transfers and indeed matched paints are available in the UK for North American railways.

When the lining and lettering is complete, a coat of varnish (from an aerosol), in gloss or semi-gloss to taste should be applied. For personal preference I do not weather coaches, except maybe for a light wash on the underframes.

Lastly, before leaving coaches, a word about my favoured method of lining, using a pen and paint. It is not as difficult as it seems or as some people would have you believe. Determination and practice will produce a satisfactory result, particularly on simple straight lines. The bow-pen, illustrated in Figure 44, is filled with paint; a cocktail stick or similar is helpful for this. The paint must be new, well stirred, and not too thick or too thin — a milky consistency. The width of the line the pen draws is governed by the screw, which adjusts the pressure on

the arch or bow element — tighter for finer lines.

Before using the pen, wipe any excess paint from the blades. The pen should be kept upright and a practice line drawn on scrap material; the thickness of the line can then be adjusted and the final line drawn with the pen against a ruler. The model should be supported to prevent it from moving, and the ruler should *not* be rested on the model, but on supports. A simple jig for this is shown in Figure 45. The trick is to keep the pen upright and draw in a steady movement, not dwelling long enough to enable the paint to blob or moving it too quickly, preventing an even flow. Like most things, practice improves the result. Remember to keep the pen clean and wash the blades in thinners between refills to keep the pen flowing freely. Curves can be drawn by this method using a template or French curves.

I paint all my coaches with car touch-up paint which is cellulose based, and line them with the above method using Humbrol enamels, which, if I make a mistake, can be wiped away without damaging the cellulose base colour. Whatever base paint you use, allow it to harden for several days before lining by the bow-pen method.

SECTION III
Buildings, road vehicles and other scenic items

In this final section, we take a look at what I call 'scenic items', comprising a whole variety of items on the model railway layout, but excluding rolling-stock and locomotives. The subjects looked at are chosen as a broad cross section to illustrate the spectrum of techniques and problems encountered in this scenic side of kit building, and the choice is not intended to be exhaustive, merely illustrative.

To start with, we will take a look at the humble plastic kits for railway buildings. They come in a bewildering variety of types and complexities, ranging from simple assemblies to more complex 'cut out yourself' packs of materials.

CHAPTER 11
Buildings

Plastic kits

Before actual construction is considered, a word or two about the preparation will not go amiss, because, as with many things, careful preparation can make a lot of difference to the finished product.

As regards tools and equipment, a craft knife or scalpel with suitable blades is essential. For general use I find the half-round-edge type preferable, whilst the chisel type is of particular use in circumstances such as the removal of moulded details, for example door handles or hand-rails. A good-quality, heavy stainless steel ruler is useful for trimming straight edges, for in some components these can be far from true. An old file, up to 8 inches in size is useful for trimming and for finishing long edges, and a small selection of cheap or old, worn needle files is useful to clean out openings such as windows and doors, and for removing all traces of 'flash'. In my experience, flat, half-round, and round cope with most situations. Finally, a pin vice and small selection of drills of say sizes 55, 60, and 65 are useful to clear any holes, or to make small holes for details added later.

Next, a word or two on the fixing of the components. We are all familiar with the tube of polystyrene cement sold to stick together aeroplane kits, but for our purposes it is best forgotten. Its use does not help in achieving a clean, accurate joint. To achieve the best results, it is necessary to use a liquid solvent applied with a small brush. There are quite a number on the market now, for example Mek Pak or Polsol. Some are principally for polystryene whilst others are designed to fasten a wider variety of plastics. Some types of plastic require the use of a specific solvent, so if you do need to stick plastics other than the straightforward polystyrene derivatives found in kits, ensure that you have the right solvent. For example, some of the 'Plastruct' moulded sections may be used to add details or in conversion work; these are moulded in ABS plastic and need a specific type of solvent, such as Plas Weld to fix them. Ask at your model shop for advice.

Some of the solvents come complete with a brush applicator as part of the cap, but these are not much use for the type of work we do. What is required is a fine brush of 00 or 0 size. The reason for this will become apparent when the method of using the solvent is described.

Before looking at actually sticking anything together, a few words on the preliminaries. You will, of course, have a clear idea of the use of the building, what its finished appearance should be, where it is to go, and how it relates to the rest of the model. Or will you? Because if we're honest with ourselves, I bet we will all at some time have bought a kit because we liked it, it was a bargain, it would fill an odd gap, or we might have received it as a present. Then we may just have wondered why it does not look quite right installed on our layout or we may wonder if we could have improved it in some way or perhaps finished off better.

What has that to do with building kits, you may ask? Well, everything and nothing. It is my belief that a great deal of time and thought needs to be given to selecting the right buildings for the layout, and here I do not mean just simply choosing any old station build-ing to use as such (there must be at least two dozen different types of station building available in OO/HO scale). You must make sure you have the right one for the model you are trying to portray. For example, look at the sta-tion on the Dignon layout. It is a straightforward, easily obtainable kit, but was chosen for its appropriateness to the model as a whole, ie the layout and the theme it portrays. It was also finished to blend in and be compatible with the other structures and scenic work on the layout and also, most importantly, to blend into the layout so that it did not look as though it had been stuck there as an afterthought. This is, in fact, more important when kits are used, as we want to avoid our building looking just like everyone el-se's and our layout looking like a pro-motional display in a department store at Christmas.

Having selected a suitable kit for the layout and for our purposes, some thought needs to be given as to how it is to be finished. Is it to have the finish

A kit of a small station building as intended by the manufacturer complete with a short length of platform, often included in European kits.

Above *The same building kit painted and altered to represent a more typical station building for a small French branch line layout. Nothing supplied with the kit has been wasted; the platform has been modified and added to the end of the building and steps made from scrap plastic. Drain pipes have been added from plastic rod. The plant growth up the wall, fairly typical of French rural stations, has been added from foliage mat on fuse wire branches and trunk. The paint finish is also deliberately weathered to avoid the appearance of a pristine building — hardly typical.*

Below *The completed building* in situ *on a layout. The dark line between the base of the goods platform ramp and the baseboard needs to be disguised with scenic dressing to give the appearance of a well-established structure.*

Careful finishing and sighting of even the simplest plastic building kits adds a new dimension. Note here the bedding in of the base of the building and platform and the character added by the climbing vegetation on the front.

that the manufacturer intended? Is it to be modified in any way? Is any interior to be fitted? Will the painting be easier before assembly? A host of possibilities need consideration before we start.

However, let us assume for now that the kit is to be built as the manufacturer intended. The first practical step comes with that old cliché, which appears on countless instruction sheets: 'Read the instructions carefully. Familiarize yourself with the parts before assembly'. Of course we all do that, don't we? Well, we should. It's no joy to be half-way through assembly to find that you cannot fit an essential part that should have been fitted earlier, or that a part has been fitted upside down or in the wrong place. I know from experience! I find it useful, therefore, to try a 'dry run' assembly of the main parts, putting them together and not fixing them with solvent but holding them in place with Blu-Tack.

This exercise serves two purposes. Firstly, it helps in the previously mentioned familiarization process, and secondly it enables the builder to ascertain how well the parts fit, and in particular whether any trimming is needed. It is important to remember here that the correct fit of the parts is the key to a well-finished model, true in shape with unsightly joints and gaps avoided. It is unusual in the modern

plastic kit for there to be much work necessary to get the main parts to fit correctly. However, Figure 46 shows how some of the common problems can be dealt with.

It is essential to the finished appearance of a building that the basic shell of a structure is square and, where there are acute angles, such as those forming a roof or dormer, that the joints at the

Typical components of a plastic construction kit for building. The components require careful removal from their carrying sprues before final assembly.

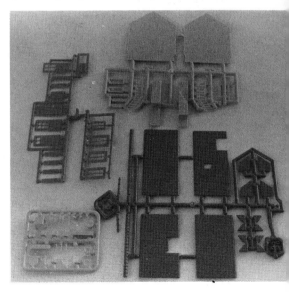

Figure 46 Checking plastic kit components

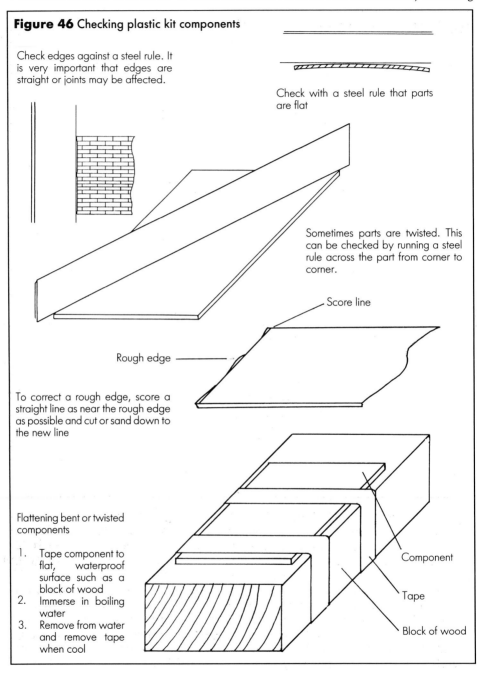

Check edges against a steel rule. It is very important that edges are straight or joints may be affected.

Check with a steel rule that parts are flat

Sometimes parts are twisted. This can be checked by running a steel rule across the part from corner to corner.

Score line

Rough edge

To correct a rough edge, score a straight line as near the rough edge as possible and cut or sand down to the new line

Flattening bent or twisted components

1. Tape component to flat, waterproof surface such as a block of wood
2. Immerse in boiling water
3. Remove from water and remove tape when cool

Component

Tape

Block of wood

Figure 47 Common methods of joining walls

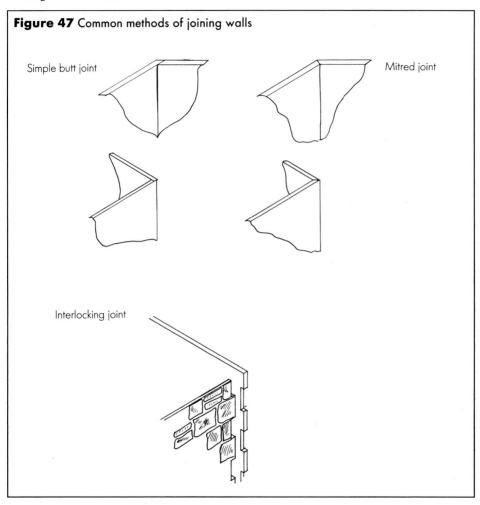

Simple butt joint

Mitred joint

Interlocking joint

angles are true and well fitting. The normal arrangements for joining the main walls of plastic building kits are shown in Figure 47. They comprise the simple butt joint, with or without the face detail of brick or stonework carried on to the edge of the moulding, the mitred corner joint, by far the most common, and the interlocking joint.

Each type of joint needs care in assembly and preparation to get the best results. For the first type it is necessary to ensure that the parts are true, and the method of checking this with a steel rule, and making the necessary adjustments, is shown in Figure 45. With this type of joint, it is necessary to try to line up courses of brick and stonework across the two walls to be joined. This is not always easy and, indeed, sometimes impossible. There are, however, ways of

Figure 48 Carrying detail round corners

Carefully cut a continuation of the mortar lines with a craft knife. For coarse stonework it may be found easier to use a knife-edged needle file.

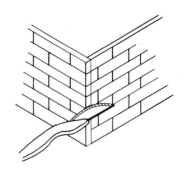

Corner joints can also be disguised with the addition of decorative corner-stones made from cartridge paper in the smaller scales, or plasticard and modelling clay in the larger scales.

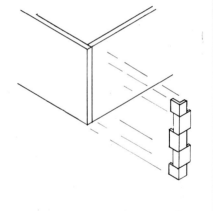

disguising this, as shown in Figure 48. Where a piece to be joined by the simple butt joint does not have the detail carried round on to the edge which will be exposed, it is a relatively simple matter to add this to the bare edge. Care is, of course, necessary to ensure that any courses of brick or stone are carried round. A sharp craft knife and steel rule are all that is required to add the course lines to the bare plastic, as shown in Figure 47. It will be easier to do this as the basic shell is being assembled but, inevitably, only two of the four corner joints can be modified at this stage in the assembly. This means that great care will be needed when working on the remaining two, as it will be difficult to support the model at the inside of the joints.

The mitred joint is the most common joint type found in plastic building kits

Figure 49 A simple angle jig

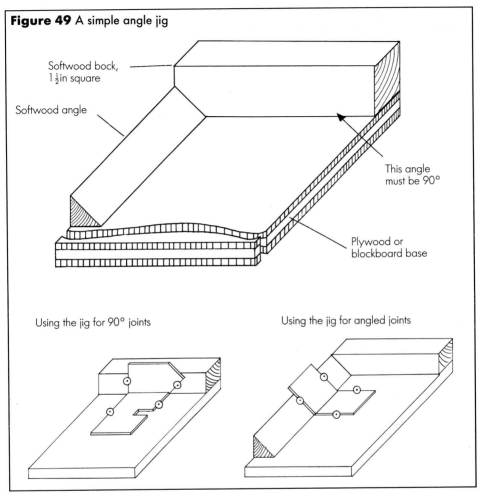

Softwood bock,
1½in square

Softwood angle

This angle
must be 90°

Plywood or
blockboard base

Using the jig for 90° joints

Using the jig for angled joints

and overcomes to a large extent the need to carry details around corners as no edges are exposed. Care is, however, necessary to ensure that such joints are square and that too much of the sometimes very fine edge which will carry the detail to the corner is not removed when trimming the parts for a final fit.

The two most common problems with this type of joint occur in lining up the details around the corner, which are sometimes not accurately aligned on the mouldings, and in ensuring a 90° joint. The first problem is dealt with in a similar manner to the carrying of detail across virgin edges as shown in Figure 48, whilst the second is a problem common to all joints, the solution for which is shown in Figure 49. The preparation of the mitred edge to obtain a 90° joint does, however,

Figure 50 Supporting mitre-edged components

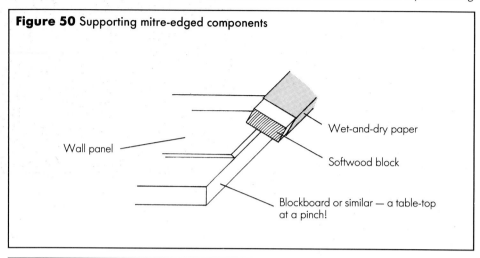

Wall panel

Wet-and-dry paper

Softwood block

Blockboard or similar — a table-top at a pinch!

Figure 51 Improving an interlocking joint

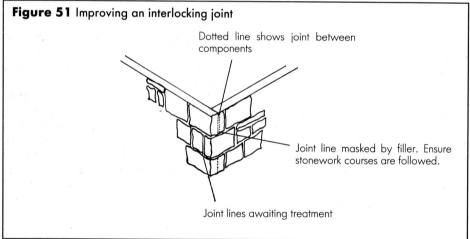

Dotted line shows joint between components

Joint line masked by filler. Ensure stonework courses are followed.

Joint lines awaiting treatment

require great care and it is a simple matter of using a fine wet-and-dry paper on a wooden block, very gently, to smooth the joint. Remember the old adage that you can always take off a little more, but you can't put it back. A helpful method of support is shown in Figure 50.

The last type of joint, the interlocking joint, seems to be most commonly associated with stonework. It is, as its name suggests, a joint where the two edges to be joined have interlocking tabs in the courses to enable them to fit together (see Figure 47). Unfortunately, this type of joint can leave unsightly gaps and problems with alignment of the courses, but these problems are quite easily dealt with as shown in Figure 51.

The need to have accurate joints in all three methods has repeatedly been mentioned because it is of paramount importance. The principle aid to this is a simple assembly block, which merely comprises a small, flat piece of block or similar board to which are added at the edges two or three pieces of softwood, a piece about $\frac{1}{2}$ in high, another 2 in high and an angled section are, I find ideal for most situations (see Figure 49). Components can then be held at 90° to each other against the angle formed by the softwood and board whilst being fixed, and a correct angle is ensured, providing, of course, that the angle between the block-board and softwood is correct to start with. Here, all that is necessary is to ensure that the softwood is itself square before it is fastened (I would suggest screwed and glued) to the blockboard base. The angled softwood is used similarly and it comes into its own for roofs and other parts which require to be fastened at an angle.

Clearly, it will not be possible in assembling four corners of a building for the procedure for each corner to be identical. There are basically two approaches, firstly, to assemble diagonally opposite corners and then the two resultant L-shaped sub-assemblies, to make the final rectangle, or to assemble two walls to one side wall, fixing the fourth wall in place last. Each kit will lend itself to its own order of assembly, depending largely on whether walls are in one piece or made up of several pieces to accommodate say, a porch. The specific kit instructions may suggest a favoured order, but more than likely you will be required to work this out for yourself. Here the preparation, 'dry run' assembly and familiarization with the model will pay dividends. Whatever assembly order

The basic four walls assembled. This kit shows a variation on the type of corner joint described in the text. A butt joint has cornerstones ingeniously moulded on to the gable end walls to disguise the joint.

you choose, remember that the assembly block aid described is very versatile and an easy way of ensuring a square accurate joint.

The use of the solvent next deserves mention. As previously stated, there are a number of types on the market, perhaps the most common being Mek Pak and Polsol. The ideal situation is for the parts being assembled to be held in place for a few seconds whilst a small amount of solvent is applied by a fine brush to the inside of the joint, the solvent flowing into the joint. Providing that it is applied sparingly and that the parts fit well and are held steady in the final position, the joint should be sufficiently well made after a few seconds for the assembly to be carefully moved, and put on one side for a while to harden off. Obviously, at this stage any strain or weight on the joint should be avoided.

Flood the joint with too much solvent and the plastic will soften, the joint will take a long time to set with the risk of distortion or damage to surface detail, and the solvent will get where you do not want it. Specifically, there is a danger of it flooding through and affecting the outer surface of the model, or, if it is picked up, finger prints may become embossed in the softened plastic which may be difficult, if not impossible, to remove. So, take care then in the use of solvents.

One advantage of assembling parts in this way is that they can, by application of further solvent, usually, and with care, be separated without too much damage, if it has been found that a mistake has been made. Hopefully, however, all the careful thought and preparation should have minimized this, possibility.

Once the basic shell of walls has been assembled, consideration needs to be given to the arrangements of doors and windows. Is any interior to be provided, doors left open, or people placed inside and, particularly, how and when is the model to be painted?

Painting is considered later in more detail, but here it is sufficient to give consideration to how the final finish will be best achieved. For example, if the building is to have a rendered finish it may be desirable to spray-paint the

shell, in which case windows, doors, etc will require adding later. I find that the spray painting of buildings is not normally necessary unless a large expanse of newly-painted rendering is to be depicted, or if it is being used as the base colour on a large expanse of brick, stone or slate work. For most purposes, therefore, in the smaller scales (2mm to 4mm) I find brush painting suffices for most situations.

However, care needs to be taken with the fitting of windows and avoiding getting the paint on to glazing. Here, my experience leads me away from following kit assembly instructions in that at this basic stage I will carry out painting work and prepare doors and windows to almost their final appearance before continuing with the construction of the main building.

Most window assemblies in plastic kits comprise of moulded window frames which are designed to be pushed into the window openings from the inside. Some, where there is considerable external bulk and detail on the frames, push in from the outside. Doors are often similarly designed.

Cut the door and window frames from their moulding sprues and clean and prepare them. Fit them into their

Door and window frames painted on their sprues, as described in the text, will fit neatly into their apertures from the inside of the building.

apertures but do not fix them. If there is any trimming or moulding flash to be removed, do so at this stage, and if there are windows and apertures which need to be trimmed so much that they become tailor-made, as it were, then carefully mark them so that when final assembly takes place you will know which frame fits which opening. A small coloured dot on the inside of a frame and another on the inside of the wall adjacent to the opening should suffice. Once this has been completed, paint the frames, ensuring that the insides of the rectangles formed by the glazing bars are fully coloured.

Most plastic kit glazing consists of fixing clear glazing strip to the inside of windows and doors, and usually this is cut from a sheet of glazing material. It is normally sufficient in the smaller scales and, indeed, fairly standard practice in kits, for the glazing material to be fixed on to the rear of the frame.

Once the window frames are thoroughly dry, cut the glazing material to the exact size of the frame and fix it to the frame around the edges. Solvent used sparingly will neither damage the painted frame nor the glazing material. Check the fit of the window assembly, trim further if necessary and put on one side.

Doorways can be similarly treated, painting and, where appropriate, glazing, and again putting on one side until the later stages of construction. Some thoughts on detailing doors are mentioned later, and it would be best to do this also before painting.

Now is the time to also consider the painting of details such as downspouts, gutters, etc, and putting these on one side for final assembly. Check first, of course, that they fit, and carry out any

Roof panels assembled on to the walls complete the basic structure. The ridge tile moulding is quite effective and hides the inevitable joint between the panels at the apex of the roof. The gap at the right-hand side is for the chimney which will be added later.

necessary trimming or enlarging of fixing holes, etc. Thoughts on detailing these fittings are mentioned later.

The roof is normally made up of large moulded panels which are fixed directly to the gable walls of the building. The roof may include a dormer which in itself is usually a sub-assembly of roof, wall and window panels, and which should be treated in the same way as the main building and added as a complete sub-assembly to the main building, usually directly on to the roof. This feature is very common on Continental kits, particularly the German period buildings. They are simple and straightforward and require little further comment.

There is an advantage in making the roof as a separate sub-assembly fixed in one piece to the main building. It is often difficult to get the joint at the roof

Figure 52 Building a roof up on barge boards for separate assembly

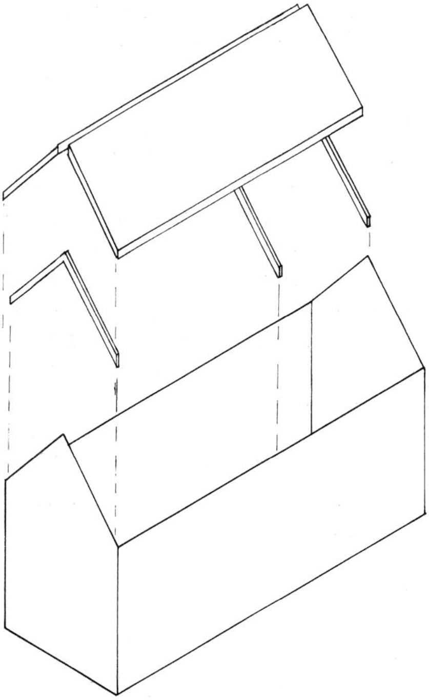

Barge-board, if provided, can be used as a template or former on which to assemble the roof panels.

Additional supports will be required and can be cut from plasticard.

If there are no exterior barge-boards, interior ones can be used using the gable end as a template. The roof then slips into the walls, the interior barge-boards locating the roof accurately, rather like a box lid.

apex right and a close fit with the main building, but it is easier if the roof is treated as a separate assembly. Also, it enables access for detailing and may in some circumstances ease painting.

If a building has separate barge-board mouldings, these can be used as the base on which the roof can be built. Check first, of course, against the gable walls that the angle of the barge-boards and their length is correct (see Figure 52). Fascia boards and, ultimately, gutters can also be added at this stage, as can any dormer or chimney detail. A long roof may require additional supports rather than just the two sets of barge-boards at the ends. These are easily cut from plasticard, say 40 thou thickness, using the bargeboards as a pattern.

If there are no barge-boards on a roof, internal supports can be cut from plasticard as described above, using the gable walls as a pattern, and the roof can be assembled on these. If these are designed to fit just inside the gable walls at either end, with perhaps additional support in the middle, then it would be possible to arrange a close-fitting, lift-off roof which, should you desire, could be removed to show off a fully-detailed interior.

Getting the angles at the apex of a roof right can be quite awkward, even with a sub-assembly as described. Unfortunately, a great many kit roofs do not have chamfered edges to facilitate a sharp, well-finished roof ridge. Invariably the model is left with a V-shaped channel where the straight edges have come together at an angle.

The assembly block or jig referred to earlier had an angled piece of softwood, and this can be used as an aid to assembling roof panels. A variation on this would be to place two triangular sections of softwood adjacent to each other as a jig, but then the angle would be fixed. The joint at the top of a real roof, whether slate, pantile or modern concrete tiles, has a similar problem, hence the addition of ridge tiles of one form or another. Most kits offer a plastic moulding to represent this and hide the joint. Care needs to be exercised in fitting this, and indeed in the construction of the roof generally, as it becomes the most visible element of the model when it is placed on a layout.

If the kit does not provide a ridge and the assembly leaves a gap or an untidy edge, or if the ridge provided does not fit, then all is not lost as it is a simple matter to put it right. It is possible to buy plastic mouldings of ridge tiles and these can be easily cut and used on the kit roof. Alternatively, it is an easy task to make your own. Figure 53 shows the simple methods of making the three most common types, for slate, pantile

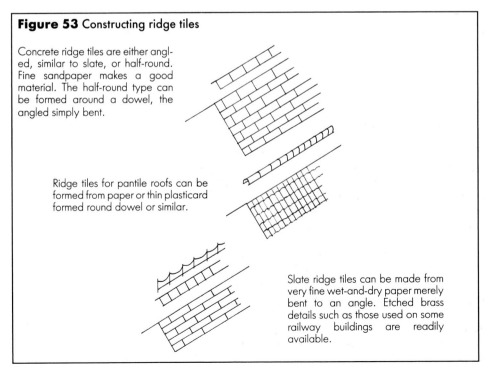

Figure 53 Constructing ridge tiles

Concrete ridge tiles are either angled, similar to slate, or half-round. Fine sandpaper makes a good material. The half-round type can be formed around a dowel, the angled simply bent.

Ridge tiles for pantile roofs can be formed from paper or thin plasticard formed round dowel or similar.

Slate ridge tiles can be made from very fine wet-and-dry paper merely bent to an angle. Etched brass details such as those used on some railway buildings are readily available.

The completed buildings in their setting on a layout. Details such as the water-trough and window boxes, complete with flowers made from foliage mat, rolled into a ball and painted with bright spots of colour to represent flowers, aid the creation of an authentic scene.

and modern concrete tile roofs. Care should be taken to ensure that your ridge tiles are in proportion to the main roofing tiles or slates — if in doubt, have a look at a real roof of that type.

Some buildings have rather ornate wrought ironwork for decoration on their ridges, and a variety of types are available as etchings. The firm of Scale Link is a good source of these and other architectural details, from wrought-iron and cast-iron clocks to classical pillars.

Before final assembly of the building, painting needs to be considered. Hav-

ing left off the doors, windows, rain-water pipes and other bits and pieces and painted these separately, attention can be turned to the main building and roof assemblies.

Starting with the main building, assuming that it is of embossed brick or stone, it is necessary to give it a once-over coat of base colour. Here you need to be quite specific with the type of brick or stone the building is made of, and this will, of course, be reflected in the geographical setting. For the purpose of illustrating techniques of finishing brickwork, let us concentrate on

A further view of the same row of buildings showing them well 'settled' into the scenic base. The small gap at the gable end between roof and wall, picked up by the camera, is barely discernible to the naked eye. Nevertheless, this type of blemish should be attended to with filler.

three main colorations. Firstly, engineers' blue brick, usually found on bridges and platform edges, common red brick (of which there are infinite colour variations) and the yellow (non-glazed) brick.

In the case of the first type, you would need to give the structure a coat of matt mid-grey which has just a shade of blue; Humbrol No 96 makes a good base. When this is thoroughly dry, the mortar courses are given a coat of cream or light grey which will inevitably spread on to the brickwork. Treat a small area at a time and wipe the mortar colour off the brickwork face with a clean cloth before it dries. When this is complete you will be left with walls which should have an overall grey-blue effect with the residue of the mortar colour left in the mortar courses. Detailing now takes place, as individual bricks are picked out in slightly varying shades of the original colour, the emphasis being on shades towards blue and purple. Broad areas can be treated by dry brushing a slightly different shade (see page 114) before a few individual bricks are picked out.

The same technique is used for red brick except that the base colour changes as do the detail colours. Red brick covers a variety of shades from almost brown to quite a bright red and, of course, the base colour needs to be chosen to suit the effect you want. Various shades ranging from pale pink-grey through orange to blue can be used for picking out individual bricks and dry brushing.

Similarly, the yellow brick base colour can be of a variety of shades from cream to almost brown. Pick out, and dry brush, with slightly differing shades based on the basic colours, but choose those that will have the effect of darkening a light base colour and lightening a dark base. Varnishing over with either satin or eggshell gives the effect of glazed brickwork.

Have a good look at brick and stone walls to see the subtle differences in colour, and the discoloration of grime, wear and water, which can all be added by dry brushing appropriate colours; dark grey, almost black, for sooty grime, or green to represent dampness and mould, adjacent, say to downspouts or under gutters.

Stonework is treated similarly to brick, but the individual stones are larger and can be treated more easily. It might sound a tedious job but the reward is well worth it and it is not half as bad as it sounds! The illustrations show the techniques involved in finishing brick and stonework.

The roof itself will require painting to represent the material it is supposed to be constructed of. Here again it is a question of picking out individual slates and tiles after a base colour has been achieved.

There is a great deal you can do to plastic kits to improve them or adapt them to your needs. Many of the improvements are common to other forms of building kits and are covered later. However, a brief word about adaptation, extension and cross-kitting is appropriate here.

The plastic kit, as it comes, is a good base and, properly finished and used, is in itself most acceptable. There will, however, be occasions where a small alteration here or there can make the kit just the thing for your needs. At its simplest, it might mean the replacement of a slate roof with a pantile roof, a very simple operation using the pan-

Figure 54 Applying overlays

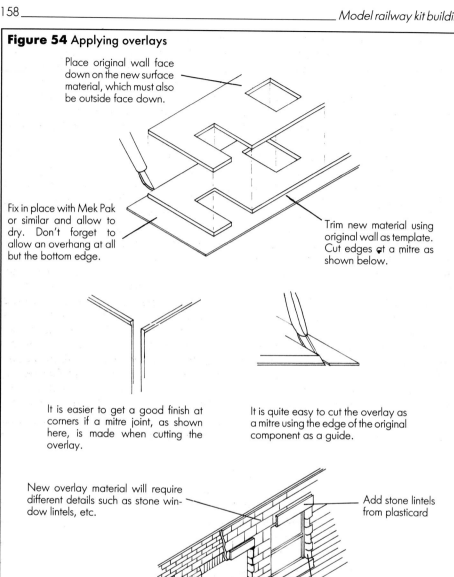

Place original wall face down on the new surface material, which must also be outside face down.

Fix in place with Mek Pak or similar and allow to dry. Don't forget to allow an overhang at all but the bottom edge.

Trim new material using original wall as template. Cut edges at a mitre as shown below.

It is easier to get a good finish at corners if a mitre joint, as shown here, is made when cutting the overlay.

It is quite easy to cut the overlay as a mitre using the edge of the original component as a guide.

New overlay material will require different details such as stone window lintels, etc.

Add stone lintels from plasticard

Decorative corner-stones can ·be added from plasticard or modelling putty

tile roof tile sheets from the Wills range, using the roof panels supplied in the kit as templates and constructing the roof as outlined earlier.

There are some kits on the market which have the walls finished in plain plastic, so a pre-printed paper stone or brick covering can be overlaid. These can look well in photographs but unconvincing on an actual model, having no relief and with usually rather garish colouring. It is simplicity itself, using the original walls as templates, to cut out embossed plasticard brick or stone with which the building can be overlaid and its appearance transformed. The overlays can be fixed with the liquid cement as solvent, the edges being left slightly longer than the originals to enable them to be mitred for a well-fitting corner joint (see Figure 54).

Equally, it is a similar operation to change stone to brick, brick to stone, or rendering to either. You could even add wooden planking or weatherboarding or you may also need to add some additional structural work, for example corner-stones, stone mullions, keystones in door and window arches, or even use the overlay to obliterate windows and doorways, perhaps cutting new ones in different positions. These are all easily achieved as shown in the diagram.

Kits can also be cut down, as, for example, some of the larger engine or goods sheds, but be careful to retain essential items such as doors, windows, goods loading platforms, etc. They can also easily be modified by the simple expedient of omitting part of the kit, for example an extension to a main building or a clerestory roof on an engine shed, and, providing the omission would be sensible and practical in the full-size version and any resultant gaps in roofs or surface detail in the model are covered, then it is an easy modification. Indeed, where the omission of an extension leaves a gap in surface detail, say on a wall, use the opportunity to create an individual feature by filling

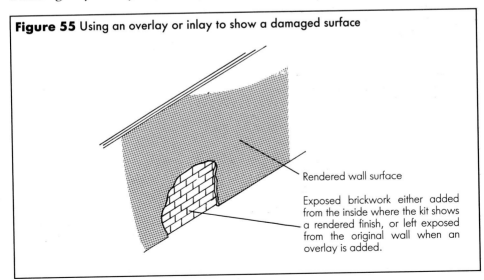

Figure 55 Using an overlay or inlay to show a damaged surface

Rendered wall surface

Exposed brickwork either added from the inside where the kit shows a rendered finish, or left exposed from the original wall when an overlay is added.

Figure 56 Arrangement for combining plastic shed kits

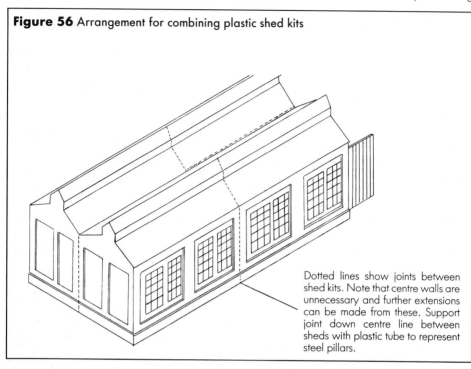

Dotted lines show joints between shed kits. Note that centre walls are unnecessary and further extensions can be made from these. Support joint down centre line between sheds with plastic tube to represent steel pillars.

the gap with a piece of balsa, suitably painted to represent the remnants of roof timbers, or brick paper or brick plasticard depending on the depth available, to show the exposed brick if it is a rendered surface, or perhaps replacement patched brickwork if it is a plain brick or stone wall. Figure 55 shows how this can be done.

It is possible to combine the components from more than one kit to enable a much larger building of the same type to be constructed, and obvious examples are combinations of factory or warehouse kits or engine sheds. By combining for example, the cheap yet realistic Dapol engine sheds, you transform this simple, small, single-road branch shed into a larger depot capable of handling more and bigger locomot-

ives. This simple example is illustrated in Figure 56, and shows how four kits could be combined.

Cardboard kits

The card building kit has been around for a long time; in its simplest and most familiar form it is perhaps illustrated by the cut-out models on the back of cereal packets or those sold at stately homes and castles as souvenirs. At its most sophisticated it is probably represented by the kits in the Prototype range, which are accurate models of specific railway buildings. Somewhere between lies the popular Superquick range of buildings which are largely pre-cut. The beauty of the better card kits is that they are pre-printed, and the colourings are quite effective. They suffer from the lack of relief detail in the brick courses, wood panelling, etc, but to some extent this can be rectified.

The essential tools for building these card kits are a good quality steel rule, a cutting board (a smooth, hard board on which cardboard can be cut), a sharp craft knife or scalpel, and a good supply of replacement blades. (It is essential in cutting cardboard to avoid leaving a feathered edge, so the knife must be sharp. The blades are soon blunted and should be replaced frequently.)

There are a variety of glues available which will stick cardboard. I prefer to use PVA woodworking glue, applied neat with a fine brush. It has the advantages of being quite strong and of drying colourless. There is now a variety available which dries quite quickly, thus speeding up construction.

The first step, as with all kits, is to read carefully the instructions supplied, and watch for the little constructional notes which appear on the carrying sheets in some kits.

Those kits with the main parts pre-cut will still require the parts to be removed from the surrounding sheet at certain points, and on no account should these be pushed or twisted free, as not only is there a risk of damaging the parts but you will almost certainly leave behind a blemish. Cut the parts out as you require them, carefully and with a sharp knife.

It is very important to familiarize yourself with the parts and intended construction methods of those kits such as the Prototype range, which require cutting out. Usually, these kits are designed to have the outer walls strengthened and supported by a lami-nated construction of several thicknesses. The laminations may be of different sizes to enable rebates to be built in to fix and locate other walls, etc. It is therefore essential that these parts are accurately aligned and cleanly cut.

Before cutting out the main parts, the outer skin with the pre-printed detail can have some relief embossed by the simple expedient of going over mortar or planking lines with a *sharp, hard* pencil of at least 2H (preferably 4) and a ruler. The effect created is quite well worth the effort. It is much easier to do this before the parts are cut out, and is quite simple, requiring good lighting, patience and a continually sharp pencil.

The simple wooden block jig shown in Figure 48 and described earlier is again a useful aid in ensuring a square assembly. Be careful to keep the timber clean, however, as the glue used to stick the cardboard will also stick the parts to the wood, and any traces left on the timber may also distort future assemblies. If the glue is used sensibly and sparingly, it should not be a problem, but if too much glue is used and it seeps out of the joints on to the face side of parts, it may damage them. Surplus glue should be carefully wiped away with a clean moist rag whilst still wet.

It is inevitable that during the construction of a cardboard kit, edges of bare, unprinted cardboard will show, and similarly there may be the odd blemish where, even in the pre-cut type of kit, parts have been removed from the surrounding cardboard. These edges can easily be disguised by colouring with a paint matching the adjacent surfaces. Make sure you use a matt paint and that it is applied carefully, and not

Above *Cardboard kits can provide a source of quite large buildings such as Heckington Station ex GNR, which is some 18 in long.*

Left *Although comparatively small and simple, the level of detail and overall appearance of the finished model belies the cardboard origins of this signal box.*

Below *The bridge shown here is entirely in cardboard but is quite strong structurally and also very adaptable — the photograph of a display model shows most permutations. (Photos Prototype Models)*

as a treacly mess! I keep an old child's water colour set, mix a stiff colouring and apply it with a fine brush. Equally satisfactory results can be obtained using coloured felt-tip pens.

As with the plastic kits dealt with earlier, the roof is very important because it is the most prominent aspect of a building once it is on the layout. Sadly, a flat card roof, however well printed and coloured, adds nothing to a model. The simplest way of improving the roof is to treat it in the same way as the brick, embossing the tiles or slates with a hard pencil, in particular the horizontal lines. It is also quite simple to build up new surface detail on the roof panels using cartridge paper to represent individual tiles — this is shown in Figure 57. New ridge tile detail can easily be made from paper

and added. This method also enables the roof material to be changed from, say, tile to slate.

Another alternative which also enables the type of roof to be changed is to use plastic roof panels. For example, Wills produce packs representing the common types of roofing materials used. These can be cut using the original roof as a template and built up on hidden plasticard interior supports as described earlier for the plastic kits.

Windows for cardboard kits generally come in two varieties, moulded plastic frames which require glazing and which fit the window and door openings, and the clear glazing sheet with a cream or white frame and glazing bars printed on. The plastic frames are treated in exactly the same way as the

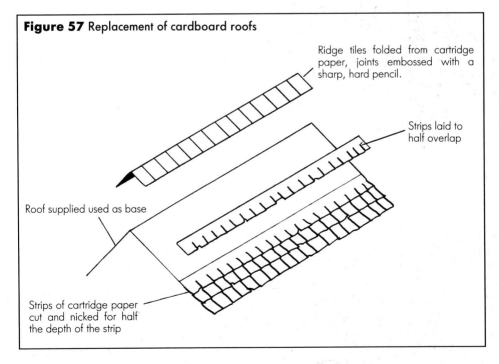

Figure 57 Replacement of cardboard roofs

Ridge tiles folded from cartridge paper, joints embossed with a sharp, hard pencil.

Strips laid to half overlap

Roof supplied used as base

Strips of cartridge paper cut and nicked for half the depth of the strip

similar doors and windows described earlier for plastic kits, and will require fixing to the card shell with UHU or a similar type of glue applied sparingly. Obviously, the door and window frames should be painted before glazing and fixing. The latter type represents the traditional approach and I do not think for most purposes it presents sufficiently detailed windows. They can be replaced either by using the pre-moulded plastic windows and doors available from, say, Peco or Faller or by fabricating your own from plastic micro-strip should you not be able to get suitable replacements ready made. The construction of replacement doors and windows in this way is shown in Figure 58.

Many of the more recent cardboard kits include details made from plastic, not only doors and windows but gutters, downspouts, steps, etc. These should be painted and allowed to dry before being applied to the main shell of the building. UHU or a similar type of glue will be needed for this and should be applied sparingly on the end of a

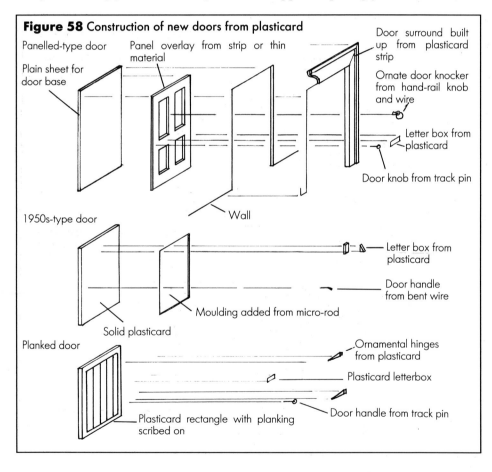

Figure 58 Construction of new doors from plasticard

Panelled-type door

Plain sheet for door base

Panel overlay from strip or thin material

Wall

Door surround built up from plasticard strip

Ornate door knocker from hand-rail knob and wire

Letter box from plasticard

Door knob from track pin

1950s-type door

Solid plasticard

Moulding added from micro-rod

Letter box from plasticard

Door handle from bent wire

Planked door

Plasticard rectangle with planking scribed on

Ornamental hinges from plasticard

Plasticard letterbox

Door handle from track pin

cocktail stick or similar implement, rather than directly from the tube, for neatness and the best results.

On those kits which still expect you to fold up details such as gutters from card, such details can be discarded and replaced with readily available plastic mouldings or etchings. There are also a number of types of chimney pots available as white metal castings, which are preferable to card fabrications, and even plastic ones included with some kits.

It is also quite easy to alter cardboard building kits, to replace brick walls with stone or rendering, or to add weather-boarding. These alterations or additions can either be accomplished in matching brick or stone papers printed on cardboard (the principal manufacturers offer matching brick, stone and slate papers) and treated in the manner described for the main kit, or by the plastic moulded panels from Slaters or Wills who between them cover most materials from rendering to corrugated iron sheets.

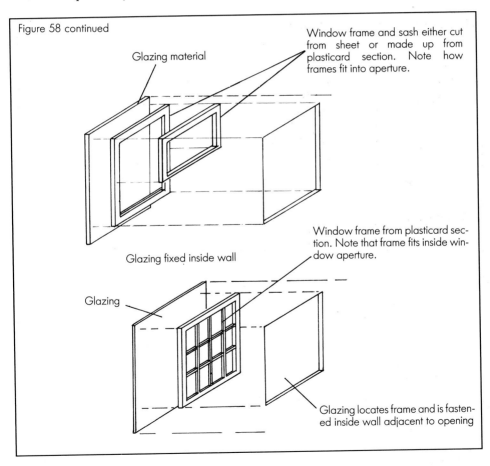

Figure 58 continued

Glazing material

Window frame and sash either cut from sheet or made up from plasticard section. Note how frames fit into aperture.

Glazing fixed inside wall

Window frame from plasticard section. Note that frame fits inside window aperture.

Glazing

Glazing locates frame and is fastened inside wall adjacent to opening

CHAPTER 12
Changing and adding details

Much of the detail on buildings, whether plastic or cardboard, can be changed and more added. Character can easily be added to give even a common kit, built as intended by the manufacturers an air of individuality. Reference has already been made to some of the changes, but a few more simple ones are suggested in the following few paragraphs and illustrated in the diagrams and photographs.

Starting with the simplest, if your layout is set in a period from the 1950s onwards, how about a TV aerial added to the roof? These are easily made from fuse wire or plastic rod, and remember the different shapes — the 'H' type of the 1950s and 60s and the modern UHF type.

The chimney pots included in kits are often inadequate plastic rods, sometimes tapering unrealistically, so why not change them for the more substantial and typically British ones available in a variety of shapes and sizes from manufacturers such as Dart Castings, Langley and Scale Link? Some kits only provide a stack and no pots, so there is no excuse for not having any! Similarly, the gutters and downspouts provided in kits may well only be plastic rod.

There are some very highly detailed castings for rainwater equipment available from Scale Link which could be used as replacements. Alternatively it is a straightforward matter to detail the parts supplied or add your own from plastic rod. Some suggestions are shown in Figure 59.

Windows are a great source of character in buildings and it is not difficult to alter the shape of a window or to put in a different style, using either a replacement etching or moulding. One of the easiest ways to add character is to install curtains or blinds behind windows. In 2mm and 4mm scales, curtains can be added by painting a suitable shape on the rear of a glazed window, and vertical blinds can be represented by drawing a series of fine vertical lines across in white or cream, closely spaced, say up to 1mm apart. For some 4mm scale applications, and certainly for O gauge, thin paper or even cloth curtains can be added inside, again before fixing. Roller-blinds can be similarly represented, whilst the Venetian type can best be depicted by fixing suitably spaced fine plastic rod to the glazing, painting it first of course. In 7mm scale you might try fixing the rod

Figure 59 Fabricating rainwater equipment

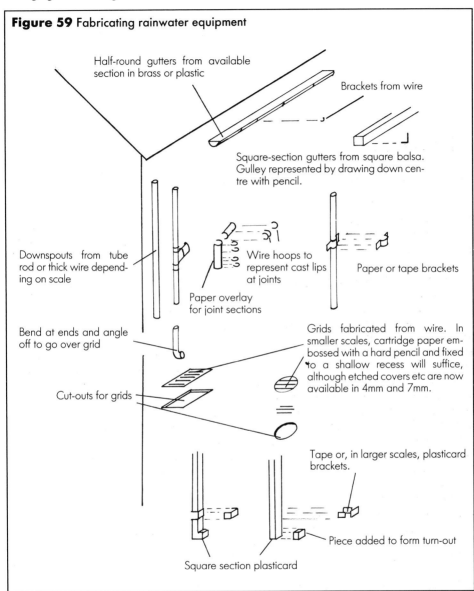

Half-round gutters from available
section in brass or plastic

Brackets from wire

Square-section gutters from square balsa.
Gulley represented by drawing down centre with pencil.

Downspouts from tube
rod or thick wire depend-
ing on scale

Wire hoops to
represent cast lips
at joints

Paper or tape brackets

Paper overlay
for joint sections

Bend at ends and angle
off to go over grid

Grids fabricated from wire. In
smaller scales, cartridge paper embossed with a hard pencil and fixed
to a shallow recess will suffice,
although etched covers etc are now
available in 4mm and 7mm.

Cut-outs for grids

Tape or, in larger scales, plasticard
brackets.

Piece added to form turn-out

Square section plasticard

to cotton or some other vertical support and suspending this inside the
window.

A broken window on a shed, out-
building or barn adds character and, if
combined with a depiction of attempts
to board and secure it, adds a nice
touch of individual realism. This is the

sort of detail that brings a model to life, and an example is shown in one of the colour photographs.

Before leaving the subject of windows, consider the humble shop, where if any representation is made of the shop interior and window display then it is usually a printed paper, one-dimensional window back. Shops, particularly the older types, have a tremendous character and can often date the period of a layout by their style, display and advertising. They cry out for detailing and the inclusion of some representation of a shop interior or display as shown in Figure 60. It is still not uncommon for small shops, particularly greengrocers, to put fruit and vegetables on display outside the shop, and this can easily be represented outside your model shop as shown in Figure 61.

It is not impossible to give a detailed

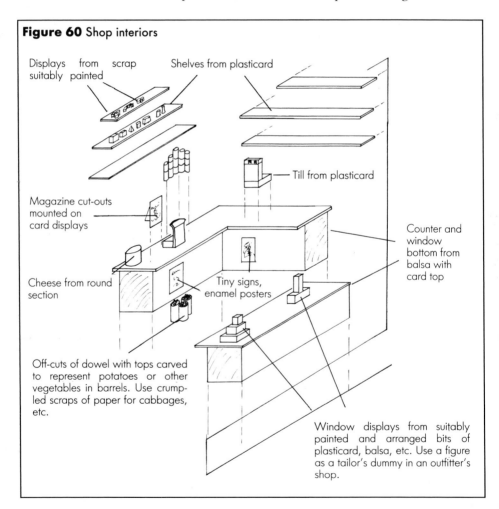

Figure 60 Shop interiors

Displays from scrap suitably painted

Shelves from plasticard

Till from plasticard

Magazine cut-outs mounted on card displays

Counter and window bottom from balsa with card top

Cheese from round section

Tiny signs, enamel posters

Off-cuts of dowel with tops carved to represent potatoes or other vegetables in barrels. Use crumpled scraps of paper for cabbages, etc.

Window displays from suitably painted and arranged bits of plasticard, balsa, etc. Use a figure as a tailor's dummy in an outfitter's shop.

interior to any building, and, in fact, there are some exquisite castings available to detail the inside of a signal box which, with its large expanse of window, really cries out for interior detailing. Full interior detail also really comes into its own for other buildings in the larger scales, in particular O gauge, where the size of window openings is large enough to enable a lack of interior to be seen. In the smaller 4mm scale, an open or part open door is easy to arrange by either simply fixing the door into its frame at an angle or, where the door frame is a single moulding, cutting round the door on three sides and scoring the fourth to enable it to be bent open.

A small scene can be incorporated behind a door left open or ajar, as shown in Figure 62, or perhaps one of the character figures available could be

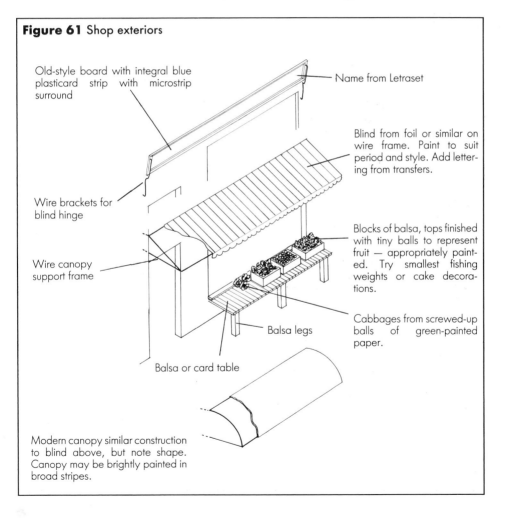

Figure 61 Shop exteriors

Old-style board with integral blue plasticard strip with microstrip surround

Name from Letraset

Blind from foil or similar on wire frame. Paint to suit period and style. Add lettering from transfers.

Wire brackets for blind hinge

Wire canopy support frame

Blocks of balsa, tops finished with tiny balls to represent fruit — appropriately painted. Try smallest fishing weights or cake decorations.

Cabbages from screwed-up balls of green-painted paper.

Balsa legs

Balsa or card table

Modern canopy similar construction to blind above, but note shape. Canopy may be brightly painted in broad stripes.

Figure 62 Detailing doorways

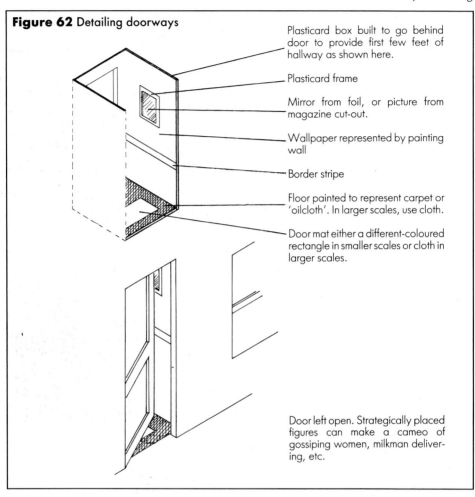

Plasticard box built to go behind door to provide first few feet of hallway as shown here.

Plasticard frame

Mirror from foil, or picture from magazine cut-out.

Wallpaper represented by painting wall

Border stripe

Floor painted to represent carpet or 'oilcloth'. In larger scales, use cloth.

Door mat either a different-coloured rectangle in smaller scales or cloth in larger scales.

Door left open. Strategically placed figures can make a cameo of gossiping women, milkman delivering, etc.

stood in the doorway gossiping. The doors themselves can have moulded door handles removed and replaced with bent wire or a small pin head.

The prominence of roofs on model buildings has already been mentioned, and some suggestions for improvements offered. Many ancillary railway and agricultural buildings, particularly since the last war, suffered from poor maintenance and some individuality

can also be offered by removing a few roof tiles and exposing the roof timbers beneath, and an example of this is illustrated amongst the colour pictures. It is an easy matter to cut round moulded (or card) tiles, remove a few in an irregular way and add some representation of roof timbers below the resultant hole. How about adding some weed growth in gutters and between ridge tiles using the coarser scenic

Right *This N gauge prize-winning model of a Lancashire and Yorkshire Railway goods shed by Peter Aldington shows the level of detail which can be achieved even in this small scale.*

Below right *Careful use of readily available 'accessories' such as barrels and other loads and, of course, people bring the model to life and are easily and inexpensively added.*

Below *Some representation of an interior where open doors or loading bays are modelled helps to establish the scene and finish a model. Here a simple representation of the interior goods platform is seen behind open doors.*

Bottom right *Rainwater goods from suitable plastic rod or tube and etched gates are some of the easily added details described in the text which add so much to a model.*

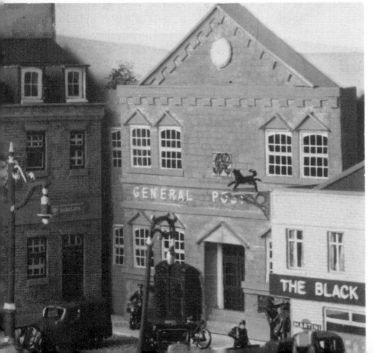

Above *This busy street scene makes the most of the many cast detailing parts available, and careful use of a commercial backscene adds depth to a narrow model. Note also the shop window detail, an easily made feature which can be built as described in the text.*

Left *There are many forms of lettering and transfers available which can be used on buildings, but don't overlook cut-outs from magazine adverts such as those for Barclays Bank and Martini shown on this busy N gauge scene.*

Figure 63 Detailing Graham Farish buildings

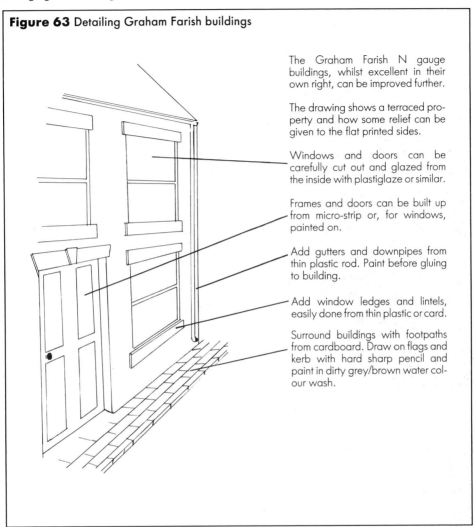

The Graham Farish N gauge buildings, whilst excellent in their own right, can be improved further.

The drawing shows a terraced property and how some relief can be given to the flat printed sides.

Windows and doors can be carefully cut out and glazed from the inside with plastiglaze or similar.

Frames and doors can be built up from micro-strip or, for windows, painted on.

Add gutters and downpipes from thin plastic rod. Paint before gluing to building.

Add window ledges and lintels, easily done from thin plastic or card.

Surround buildings with footpaths from cardboard. Draw on flags and kerb with hard sharp pencil and paint in dirty grey/brown water colour wash.

materials, an etched weather-vane or even a cast seagull or two?

Lastly on the subject of buildings, I think special reference is needed to those N gauge kits produced by Graham Farish which comprise printed cardboard overlays fitting round plastic boxes. The quality of detail and colour on the card overlays is excellent and for general use they are most acceptable. I think they deserve some detailing if they are to be used in prominent locations, with some easily added separate details to give relief. You could take this as far as replacing doors and windows, cutting out apertures in the box. Some suggestions for detailing are shown in Figure 63.

CHAPTER 13
Bridges and tunnels

The construction of bridges and tunnels requires a few comments. The general principles outlined for buildings on the preparation and joining of plastic components apply equally here, as do the comments on painting and finishing brick and stonework. I will, therefore, confine my comments to installing the structure and finishing any ironwork.

Both bridges and tunnel mouths will require careful selection to be suitable for the job you require them to do, and will also require consideration at baseboard and scenic design stage. It is usual to fix bridges to fit into gaps carefully designed and corresponding in height and length to the kit it is proposed to use. Care here will solve many problems later in fixing the bridgework, laying the track over and, of course, running.

Whilst it is possible to buy kits for complete bridges, they can often be built from plastic girders, which will require the supports or piers, also available in kit form. It is important to use the components in a way which is correct from a civil engineering point of view, and the reader can do no better

To be effective, a tunnel entrance must look as though it belongs in the landscape and is not merely stuck on the baseboard.

A small bridge such as that shown here, carrying the railway over a small watercourse, is quite effective. The scene is enhanced by the stone supports which are well bedded into the adjoining landscape.

than refer to the excellent book *Bridges for Modellers* by L.V. Wood (OPC).

It is important that, a tunnel portal looks as though it actually is the entrance to a tunnel rather than a cutting with a roof, and the surrounding scenic work is designed to achieve this. Many tunnel entrances also incorporate drainage culverts, and these can easily be built into the surrounding scenery to help give the illusion of reality.

The general procedures outlined for finishing brickwork and stone walling apply also to bridge and tunnel work, but some attention needs to be given to weathering the masonry to take into account dampness and water seepage — dry brushing with suitable greens will do the trick. Apply soot marks to overbridges and tunnel mouths where the smoke from locomotives has left stains, although clearly this will not be required if your layout is in the post-steam era.

Dry brushing ironwork with a rusty colour will leave a deposit on raised detail which will give the impression of rust. Similarly, the use of black/blue hues can give the impression of grease

on, say, a bridge expansion joint. Have a look at the real thing for some ideas.

One final point on bridge and tunnel work is to ensure that your model is actually fitted into the landscape, particularly at its base, and that it does not appear merely to have been added as an afterthought. Similar criteria and methods as shown for buildings apply here, and some examples are illustrated.

It was common practice until the late 1960s for plate girder bridges carrying a railway over a road to be painted with advertisements; those for Lanry household bleach and Ferodo brake parts, red and white on a gloss black background, spring to mind, and I recall others on ochre and orange-coloured backgrounds. It was usual for the whole bridge side to be painted the background colour, and the usual style of lettering or emblem for the product being advertised to be used. This can easily be represented on the model using transfers from the Mabex range intended to adorn road vehicles, and would make an eye-catching and authentic detail for your layout.

CHAPTER 14
Installation and final finish

The main point to remember in installing structures on the layout is that buildings generally grow out of the ground from foundations dug into it. Don't just plonk down a building on its resting spot — it will appear like something which has landed from outer space! Buildings and major engineering structures need to mimic the real thing and appear solid and well rooted. There are a number of ways of achieving this, and the simplest, assuming a level site such as a station platform or road, is to paint with a fine brush a thin line of PVA glue at the joint line where the

building and the ground meet and to sprinkle this with scenic scatter material, the same as the surrounding surface, with a few specks of a suitable green added to represent weeds.

If the building is to be on a roadside or is to have a footway around it, then the footpath can be cut to fit exactly around the building (or in front in a street scene) and the building slotted behind; any slight gaps can be given the above mentioned weed treatment, using suitable green scatter material or coarse foliage on bigger gaps.

Where structures such as platelayers'

The setting of the buildings, enhanced by the creation of an ill-kept smallholding across the road, helps to give an authentic feel to this model of rural France. The careful use of simple, readily available materials, buildings and animal figures is all that is needed.

Above *Careful attention to detail and the use of features such as the bicycle leaning on the lampost, the 'mechanicien' leaning on the brickwork reading* La Monde *and the onlooking 'fermier' all add life to this French layout.*

Below *A number of features mentioned in the text are illustrated here. The wagon is lightly weathered and the brick courses on the wall painted and high-lighted, adding a realistic dimension to moulded plastic brickwork. The masonry is bedded well into the baseboard, and the addition of scenic dressing to form weed growth at the base adds further to the impression of reality.*

Buildings on their own do not create a scene. Careful observation by the modeller helps in creating an authentic enviroment for buildings. Of particular note here is the unkempt undergrowth in the relatively inaccessible area between the stone hut and the shed, the grindstone wheel and upturned wheelbarrow, cobbled roadway and horse-drawn vehicle.

huts or bridge piers are out of the way, they are often surrounded by quite vigorous undergrowth, and this is easily represented by coarse turf or foliage mat stuck around the base of the structure. In the case of the former, do not forget the pathway to the hut and the clutter of old oil drums, grindstone and platelayers' tools, all available at low cost from the Cooper Craft range.

Mention has already been made of painting these structures, and particularly of finishing the brick and stonework and the technique of dry brushing. In general, when painting structures look

at the colours actually used to finish wood and ironwork on buildings. It is possible to be very accurate with the colours used for railway buildings many years ago, thanks to the work of dedicated researchers and books such as *Midland Style* and *Great Western Way* published by the Historical Model Railway Society, which your library should be able to obtain for you and which contain a wealth of detail on the old railway companies, from the uniforms of 'company servants', as employees.were often called, to the colours of buildings and lamps. There are many sources of

Another view of the same scene, showing the effective finishing of the stonework on the hut, the representation of mortar courses on the brick-built engine shed and the weathering near the bottom of the drain pipe, all carried out as described in the text.

this kind of information; for example, *LNWR Portrayed* by J.K. Nelson (Peco) gives details of the LNWR, whilst Ian Allen publish inexpensive guides to the four pre-nationalization companies. The leading model paint manufacturers include matched colours in their ranges for the most popular companies — so there is little excuse for getting the colour wrong. The Appendix lists a few books which could prove useful in providing prototype information.

Remember that even though a newly-painted wooden door on your house may have a high gloss, a door finished in a high gloss on a small-scale model will look wrong. As a general rule, stick to matt paints. Ensure that they are thoroughly stirred and, if using bright colours, tone them down on the model by either using a shade slightly less bright or adding a touch of grey.

Some very subtle effects of shading and weathering can be achieved by dry brushing, not only to suggest mould growth and damp patches on masonry but also on woodwork and metal fittings to give the effect of faded and damaged paintwork, and the shiny polish on, say, a hand-rail where the hands grabbing it

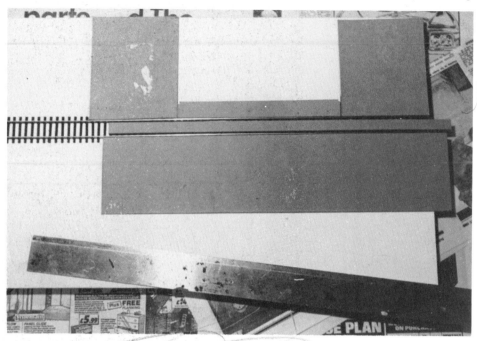

Above *The new 'ground' is carefully prepared to go around the buildings which slot into the resultant gaps.*

Below *The first stage in providing a raised ground level around a building, using card glued to the baseboard.*

A view of the completed scene. Notice the subtle shading of the stonework and the mortar courses, picked out as described in the text.

have worn a shine. Dry brush greys on the woodwork and silver or gun metal on the metal rail.

Finally, do not be tempted to use old paint which is starting to harden, as the chances are that the finish will be poor. Small tins of paint are not expensive. Also, use the best quality brushes you can afford, sable or sable substitute if you can, because, properly looked after, they will last a long time and keep their point, which is essential for accuracy in painting to a line. Keep them clean, remember not to rest them on their points and store them in an airtight container to avoid them becoming dusty.

CHAPTER 15
Road vehicles

No model railway is complete, surprisingly though it may seem, without some representation of a road vehicle, even if it is only a trailer or cart idly rotting in a yard.

For our purposes, road vehicles can be conveniently divided into self-propelled types, such as cars, buses, steam lorries, etc, and the horse-drawn type, and broadly into plastic and white metal as the basic construction materials of the many kits available.

There is an extensive range of vehicle kits, aimed at the railway modeller, particularly in 4mm scale, covering everything from a steam ploughing engine to a modern articulated lorry; they are largely white metal, but with an increasing number of plastic kits being produced. Similarly, there is an extensive and growing range of horse-drawn vehicles, highly detailed and almost exclusively in white metal, from manufacturers such as Dart Castings and Langley. And if that is not enough, there is a tremendous range of military vehicles in 1/72nd scale, which can be drawn on for 3.5mm or 4mm scale layouts, and some of these vehicles make excellent models for conversion. Indeed, many vehicles sold by the military were and still are bought and converted to other purposes by their new owners.

The comments in the previous section relating to the suitability of chosen subjects to a specific model railway layout are appropriate to road vehicles. A Ford Anglia would look somewhat incongruous on a layout set in the pre-war years, as would a steam ploughing engine next to a modern combine harvester. Road vehicles, together with buildings and people, are very important in creating an impression of period and even location, and are essential contributors to the atmosphere a model railway creates, be it a full-blown layout or a simple diorama.

Plastic kits

The contents of typical plastic road vehicle kits are illustrated here, and as can be seen there are usually considerably more parts than in the average building kit. The parts are likely to be, on the whole, quite small, often the cabs and chassis of the lorries, for example, being constructed from several pieces.

The first stage is always to check the parts, read the instructions and familiar-

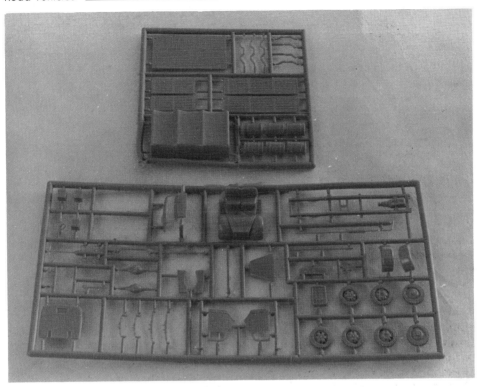

The typical contents of a plastic road vehicle kit.

ize ourselves with the beast we are to construct. If you intend any modification, then consideration will need to be given at this stage. There are some quite remarkable conversions and, until comparatively recently, almost all commercial vehicles on post-war British 4mm scale layouts seemed to be variations of the old Airfix AEC Matador truck. However, there are now considerably more types of vehicles available, and unless you are particularly interested in road vehicles it is likely that you will find something for your purposes which will suffice with minimum, if any, modification. Some easy changes and adaptations are illustrated later, but detailed rebuilding and con-

versions are beyond the scope of this book. Readers interested in this aspect may refer to the specialist magazines and books listed in the Appendix.

Getting down to actual construction, and assuming that the model is to be built as intended by the manufacturer, the first job, when we know what we are doing, is to remove the parts from the sprues with a sharp craft knife. It is preferable, to avoid losing or confusing parts, to remove them only as they are required. The parts encountered in this type of kit are likely to be much more delicate and of more complex, awkward shapes than those in buildings, and some thought concerning cutting the parts from their sprues is needed. If the parts are simply attacked unsupported, it is quite likely that the more delicate ones will snap or bend more easily than their tie to the sprue. To avoid this, ensure a sharp craft knife is used and support the sprues where they are cut with scraps of timber or by manoeuvring the sprue on the work bench or table, as illustrated.

Assembly is again with a liquid cement or solvent, applied with a fine brush into the joint. Some main body and chassis components will form 90° joints and need holding square. For parts such as lorry backs and sides, the wooden block shown in Figure 48 and described earlier is a useful aid. Improvization can similarly provide support for the more awkwardly shaped parts which need to be held at obscure angles. Blu-Tack, scraps of timber, dowelling and odd bits of packaging can often be pressed into use.

Some consideration also needs to be given to glazing and providing any interior detail before final assembly, otherwise access to cab interiors and the like may be impossible. Glazing is straightforward using clear plastic glaze and is most easily done after painting, but

Many components for road vehicle kits are anything but flat and, being often quite fragile, need supporting whilst being cut from the plastic sprue.

Well-detailed plastic kits of road vehicles are readily available and easily modified. The simple cutting away of part of the lorry to indicate an open drop-side adds life to the situation of the model, showing it in use rather than just 'plonked down' and immobile on the road, and helps to create a nice 'cameo' on a layout.

with the glazing prepared before the parts containing the window apertures are assembled. It is possible, using a very sharp pencil, to mark the shape of the aperture through on to plain paper and for this to be used as a template to cut the windows from the plastic glazing material. This process is tedious and difficult for small windows, but is worth the trouble on large ones, such as windscreens and coach or bus windows. The usual method is merely to locate strips of glazing on the inside of the vehicle, across the windows.

White metal kits

White metal kits are common and cover similar ranges to plastic kits. They can be quite simple, such as the pick-up truck illustrated, which consists merely of six parts, or more complex and highly detailed. There is nothing to fear in the assembly of these kits. The procedures to be followed are exactly

The simplest of white metal road vehicles comprise only few parts, such as the Morris Minor pick-up truck shown here. This has a one-piece cast body, a one-piece chassis/floor and four wheels and is shown stripped down in preparation for a repaint.

those outlined for plastic kits, although some of the techniques vary because of the material used.

White metal is a lead-based alloy, its exact composition depending on the job it is used for. It is invariably cast using centrifugal force into rubber-based moulds, which are formed around masters of the component to be cast. The quality of the finished casting depends on the quality of the master used, because however good the quality of the metal or however well it is cast, it can only copy the master. It also depends on the right grade of metal being used for the job to be cast. The overall quality of the kit will also depend on how well it was designed. This manufacturing process has been an invaluable boon to railway modellers and has developed significantly since it started in the 1950s. It enables the relatively small number of models

needed in a production run for the hobby to be produced at affordable prices.

The tools needed for white metal road vehicle kits are quite basic: old needle files and a craft knife with a blunted blade (a good reason to keep the blades replaced after cutting out card and plastic kit parts), some fine wet-and-dry paper, a fibreglass burnishing tool with a supply of refills and some filler such as Milliput.

White metal parts can be assembled using a low-temperature melting point solder or glue. For the comparatively small size of components in 2mm and 4mm scale road vehicles, I would recommend the use of a cyanoacrylite glue, or 'superglue' as it is colloquially known, rather than solder. The parts will need to be cleaned, any surplus metal (flash) removed carefully with the files or a craft knife used as a scraper, and the parts rubbed vigorously with the burnishing tool to smooth the surface to a finish.

The first major difference between white metal and plastic kits is apparent in the fit of the parts. Great care is needed to ensure that white metal parts fit cleanly and accurately together, and time spent at this stage ensuring a good fit is essential to achieve a well-finished model. Use the files, craft knife and wet-and-dry to trim the parts to get a good fit.

There will be occasions when a completed joint needs attention. Perhaps a locating lug is too long, and this is easily 'fettled' using the files and wet-and-dry, and finishing with the burnishing tool. More commonly there will be small gaps. These will require filling prior to painting and this is easily achieved with Milliput, a two-part epoxy filler which dries very hard and can be smoothed with wet-and-dry and the burnishing tool. I cheat a little here and smooth the still unset filler with an old craft knife blade dipped in water, which makes the final finishing when dry minimal. Be careful when using filler not to cover neighbouring detail and, when using the burnishing tool, not to rub away raised detail such as rivets.

The wooden blocks and improvisation discussed earlier as aids to square assembly and support are equally applicable with white metal kits, but beware as the assemblies are considerably heavier than their plastic counterparts.

CHAPTER 16
Painting and detailing vehicles

Considering plastic kits first, painting should be carried out before locating the windows, and this may necessitate assembling, painting and glazing a truck cab before final assembly on to the chassis and the rest of the vehicle. Any details which need to be fitted later, such as door mirrors, etc, which are better left until final assembly, can be painted later.

Painting can either be by spraying or brush. I have quite successfully used car aerosol touch-up sprays on plastic models, and providing the colour is ghosted on in light coats, rather than one thick one, there is no apparent damage to the plastic. There are also now mini-sprays of enamel paint in a growing range of colours.

Brush painting is not difficult and good results can be achieved, providing a few points are adhered to. Matt or at most semi-matt paint is required, and it should be fresh — do not use old tins. This is particularly important where large body panels are to be painted. Also use good quality brushes, the best you can afford, such as sable or artificial sable substitute. Those sold under the Inscribe label are, I have found, not too expensive and provide good results,

Usually you will find that a brush slightly bigger than you think you should use will do a good job and, holding more paint, will be easier to use.

Use the paint thoroughly stirred and thinned, building up the colour in two or three light coats rather than a single coat. Ensure ample time, usually overnight, is allowed between coats, and store the model in a clean box to protect the drying paint from dust. Details such as door mirrors and headlight lenses can be painted with well-stirred paint straight from the tin in most cases.

For preference, I usually paint the vehicle, if construction will allow, in different sections. The chassis is given an overall coat of matt black and a very thinned-down rust smeared over the main chassis girders and engine block. Details can then be picked out in appropriate colours, wheel centres in the body colour, exhaust pipes in track colour or rust, etc. The main body is usually painted a single colour, with any two tone or small areas of colour added later with a brush. Paint the lighter colour first as it makes it easier to cover any mistake with the darker colour from an adjacent body panel than

Two examples of models built from simple plastic kits. The ploughman's engine has been detailed and a representation of the motion added. The wheels have been dirtied as this model will be part of a scene on a layout showing the engine at work. When on the layout, ropes (cotton) will be coiled round the drum and run to the ploughs.

vice versa. For large areas, such as the common two-tone effects on buses or coaches, use masking tape, ensuring that it is well pressed down over any raised detail.

Certain effects can be created on the bodywork of vehicles to make them appear to 'live' on the layout. The planking of any wooden floor or sides can be dry brushed with matt khaki and browns; I find Humbrol nos 72 and 66 very useful. Handles and grab-rails can be similarly treated with gun metal or silver to show where constant use has burnished the metal. Tyres can be given a thin wash of brown/grey to show dirt, and the underside of vehicles and lower body panels treated with this to show where grime has been deposited from wheel spray and splashes from the road.

Windscreen wipers can be added from fuse wire or those sold to detail diesel locomotives could be used. The window can be dirtied and the area cleaned by the wipers left sparkling quite easily, using the same colour wash referred to above and masking the area swept by the wipers. The masking can easily be removed after the wash is dry. A flat could be filed on the bottom of a wheel to represent a flat tyre, and a cameo built around the changing of the wheel.

Wagon loads themselves are an interesting challenge. How often on layouts at an exhibition or in the model press do you see lorries with authentic loads? Timber, stone, barrels and milk churns can easily be added to open lorries, and a tarpaulin-covered load on a flat truck can be easily simulated as shown in Figure 64.

Lorries are not the only commercial vehicles, and steam provided the power for many operations; steam showman's, ploughing and traction engines are available in both plastic and

Figure 64 Lorry loads

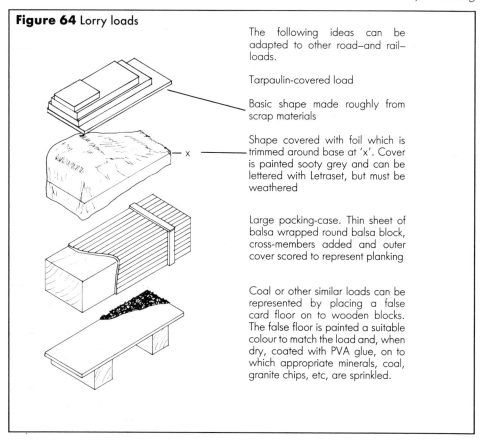

The following ideas can be adapted to other road–and rail–loads.

Tarpaulin-covered load

Basic shape made roughly from scrap materials

Shape covered with foil which is trimmed around base at 'x'. Cover is painted sooty grey and can be lettered with Letraset, but must be weathered

Large packing-case. Thin sheet of balsa wrapped round balsa block, cross-members added and outer cover scored to represent planking

Coal or other similar loads can be represented by placing a false card floor on to wooden blocks. The false floor is painted a suitable colour to match the load and, when dry, coated with PVA glue, on to which appropriate minerals, coal, granite chips, etc, are sprinkled.

white metal kits. These vehicles deserve some special mention, particularly with regard to their finishing and detailing. Addition of some representation of the valve gear on the simpler kits is an easy job with scrap plasticard and rodding, as is the addition of coal. Oil cans and tools sold for 4mm scale locomotives can also easily be added.

The painting of these vehicles requires the same basic consideration as any other road vehicle, but the addition of oil streaks of gloss black/blue, polished metal on valve gear, grease on gears, coal stains in the 'cockpit' and rust/

black burn marks on backheads, will add realism. The wheels of road rollers may be quite shiny, burnished from use. Other engines with rubber treads or tyres will need those parts painting black, whereas a ploughman's engine, in use on the farm, will need to show mud and dirt on the wheels and splashed on the underside of the boiler, cable drum, etc. This is easily represented with thin washes of the appropriate colours as described earlier for other road vehicles.

Ploughman's engines, traction engines and road rollers were often green or maroon in colour with lining in yellow, gold or white. Showman's engines, reflecting their purpose and status, carried elaborate lining, lettering and painting. Use can be made here of the lining transfers made for model railway locomotives and coaches, so you do not need to be an expert with paintbrush and lining-pen. Use the preparations now available to ensure that the transfers lie down well over the raised detail, and finish with a protective coat of spray varnish from one of the mini-sprays. Avoid high gloss, even though the most humble engine was usually well polished and cared for, as it will not look right on small scale models. A satin finish I find gives a good representation. When all is painted and finished, do not forget to add driver, buckets, hoses, tools, and all the other paraphernalia found on these wonderful machines.

The procedure for painting and finishing white metal kits is somewhat different from that of plastic kits. The model should, of course, be properly finished, smoothed and cleaned. It is important that the surface of the model is de-greased, and here the traditional method is to lightly scrub the model with detergent and an old tooth-brush, although I prefer to clean the metal with lighter fuel applied with a soft cotton pad. The fuel quickly evaporates and leaves a clean, grease-free surface on which to apply paint. Be careful, for the fuel ignites very easily and has pungent and dangerous fumes.

The model will then need priming, and ordinary car aerosol primer takes some beating. Apply in a well ventilated room and be careful not to spray too thick a coat in one go. If you have an airbrush, there are excellent primers on the market specially formulated for such use. The primer should be allowed to dry thoroughly and the model touched as little as possible. The primer will show up any flaws, and now is the time to rectify any surplus or deficiencies of materials with the wet-and-dry or filler respectively. Follow this with a further light coat of primer.

The model can then be given its main coat, again either by spray or brush application, and final effects and small details finished by brush, as appropriate, in different colours.

CHAPTER 17
Horse-drawn vehicles

The subject of horse-drawn vehicles, I appreciate, covers a wide area, but thankfully I think there are now sufficient kits of specific types in 2mm and 4mm scale by Langley and Dart Castings to serve most purposes. A nucleus of a range is also being developed in 7mm scale. Clearly, those in 2mm scale, whilst well detailed, cannot approach their larger cousins which are, particularly in 7mm scale, sufficiently detailed to form showcase models in their own right.

Like any other kit, they must be used and finished correctly. Remember that horse-drawn vehicles are not just Victorian or Edwardian but were in use in to the 1960s as milk floats, and I remember in my home town also for the delivery of meat — a sort of mobile butcher's shop. Indeed, they are making a comeback on brewer's drays in many urban areas.

The kits are usually white metal and of few components and easy assembly. Take care in assembly, though, and ensure that the parts are fitted correctly and accurately together as discussed earlier for other road vehicles.

The key to success with horse-drawn vehicles is really in the finishing and detailing. The harness is usually cast on the horse and providing that this is correct for the vehicle then it should be left. Improvement to the harness is virtually impossible in 2mm scale except for the addition of reins from fine cotton or fishing line. In 4mm scale and larger we can begin to look at adding detail and making improvements. Reins are easy to add, in 4mm from lengths of black draughtsman's lining tape, no more than $\frac{1}{2}$mm wide, while in 7mm scale 1mm tape can be used. Buckles, brasses and other metal work on harness was usually kept well cleaned and polished, even on the most mundane of vehicles, and this is easily represented by touches of appropriate metallic paint in the correct places on the harness or cast-in detail. An odd piece of wire, nickel silver for preference, can be added to represent the polished part. Coaching bits invariably had long shanks, and these can be represented easily in 7mm scale and just about in 4mm scale.

The horse itself should be painted carefully. Horses are not a uniform colour and certainly in the larger scales repay careful attention. The illustration shows the difference between a once-

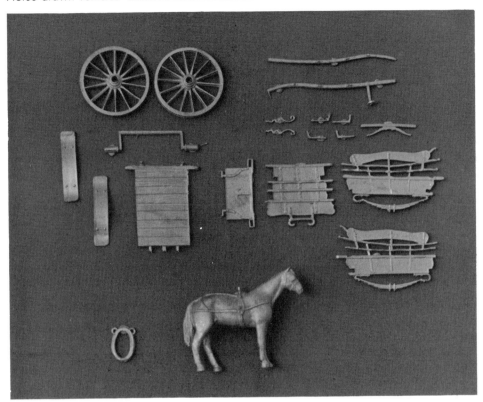

The white metal components of the Dart Castings farmer's trap kit showing excellent detail.

over of one colour and careful painting in more detail. Matt paint should, of course, be used. In some applications, such as on a horse-drawn hearse, the leather harness had a patent leather look and here gloss black will give the right finish.

Many agricultural vehicles had characteristics peculiar to their region and for an authentic, accurate setting, the correct type of vehicle is essential. Colour schemes were also quite localized, with certain body colours and lining detail being characteristic of certain counties. For example, blue with red wheels was common in the south-west, and deep golden yellow with red wheels in the eastern counties. Quite elaborate and fine lining was often carried, together with the farmer's name, or the name of the farm, dairy, etc, carried in the panels on the vehicles. Ironwork was almost exclusively black, though springs were often painted to complement the body colours. There are a number of books from which further details can be obtained, and the Appendix lists some.

Vehicle tyres may well be either rubber or steel and require painting

Figure 65 New bodies for horse-drawn vehicles

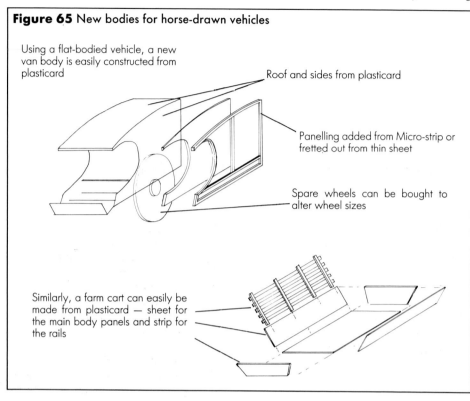

Using a flat-bodied vehicle, a new van body is easily constructed from plasticard

Roof and sides from plasticard

Panelling added from Micro-strip or fretted out from thin sheet

Spare wheels can be bought to alter wheel sizes

Similarly, a farm cart can easily be made from plasticard — sheet for the main body panels and strip for the rails

either black or silver accordingly. The lining referred to is virtually impossible in 2mm scale, not easy to achieve except on large panels in 4mm scale and requires care, with either OO loco and coach lining transfers or bow-pen and ink, in 7mm scale. If in doubt, it is best left rather than attempted and the model spoiled. Names and other lettering can be added from Letraset or similar transfers, which are available in a variety of styles and colours.

It is not only agricultural vehicles which show a local variation. Whilst the railway companies had vehicles ostensibly for the same purpose, the company variations of detail, let alone livery, make them just as distinctive as lorries and rolling-stock. Be careful, therefore, if you wish to achieve authenticity for your layout. It is often a comparatively simple matter to modify the available kits. New bodies can easily be fabricated, and the general technique involved is shown in Figure 65.

References to photographs are often the only means of establishing accuracy and books such as the OPC Miscellany series as well as specialist books are invaluable here.

Appendix — Further reading

Magazines

For kit conversions and super-detailing:
Railway Modeller
Scale Model Trains
Finescale Modeller
For kit building and improving, particularly locomotives and rolling-stock:
Model Railways
Model Railway Journal

Books

Locomotives

An Illustrated History of LMS Locomotives, Jenkinson & Essery, OPC and Silver Link
An Illustrated Review of Midland Locomotives, Jenkinson & Essery, Wild Swan
Highland Railway Locomotives, P. Tatlow, OPC
Pictorial Record of Great Western Engines, J. Russell, OPC
An Illustrated History of LNWR Locomotives, E. Talbot, OPC
LSWR Locomotives, D.L. Bradley, Wild Swan
'Locomotives' series by B. Haresnape, Ian Allan:
Stanier Locomotives
Fowler Locomotives
Churchward Locomotives
Collett & Hawksworth Locomotives
Bulleid Locomotives
Maunsell Locomotives
Stroudley Locomotives
Ivatt & Riddles Locomotives
Robinson Locomotives

RCTS Locomotive History Series on LNER, GWR, South Eastern, SECR, LCDR, Isle of Wight, GNR — authoritative detailed texts on locomotives, but few pictures.

Rolling-stock

An Illustrated History of Southern Wagons, OPC
LNER Wagons, P. Tatlow, OPC
Midland Wagons, 2 Volumes R.J. Essery, OPC
The LMS Wagon, Essery & Morgan, David & Charles
Bulleid Coaches in 4mm Scale, S.W. Stevens-Stratton, Ian Allan
Historic Carriage Drawings in 4mm Scale, Vol I, Jenkinson & Campling, Ian Allan
Midland Carriages — An Illustrated Review, Jenkinson & Essery, OPC

Midland Carriages, 2 Volumes, G. Dow, Wild Swan

LMS Coaches, Essery & Jenkinson, OPC

An Illustrated History of LNWR Carriages, Jenkinson, OPC

Road Vehicles

Road Vehicles of the GWR, P.J. Kelley, OPC

A Pictorial Record of LMS Road Vehicles, Twells & Bourne, OPC

The British Bus, Gavin Booth, Ian Allan

The Leyland Bus, Doug Jack, Transport Publishing Co

Vintage Lorry Album, edited by Nick Baldwin, F. Warne (several volumes)

The Story of the Steam Plough Works (John Fowler & Co, Leeds), M.R. Lane, Northgate Publishing

Making Model Trucks, G. Scarborough, Patrick Stephens Ltd

How to Go Car Modelling, G. Scarborough, Patrick Stephens Ltd

World Trucks Series, Partick Stephens Limited

Traction Engines in Close Up, E.H. Sawford, D. Bradford-Barton

Burrell Showmans Road Locomotives, M.R. Lane, MAP

Farm Wagons and Carts, J. Arnold, David & Charles

Farm Trucks in Colour, M. Williams, Blandford Colour Series

General

Bridges for Modellers, L.V. Wood, OPC

LNWR Portrayed, J.K. Nelson, Peco

Modellers' Guide to the LNER, David Adair, Patrick Stephens Limited

HMRS publications on varied details from locomotives to uniforms:

> *Midland Style*
> *Great Western Way*
> *Livery Register LSWR & Southern Railways*

OPC 'Miscellany' series, photographic records of varied aspects of the companies from locos and stock to buildings:

> *GWR*
> *LNWR*
> *LMS*
> *Lancashire and Yorkshire*

This list is by no means exhaustive, but serves to illustrate some sources of information available to the modeller.

Index

Other top model railway books from PSL

SIMPLE MODEL RAILWAY LAYOUTS
by T.J. Booth
For all modellers who believe that they have no room in their homes for a model railway, here are ten simple but effective layouts on baseboards as small as 8ft × 1ft to prove them wrong.

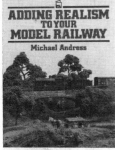

ADDING REALISM TO YOUR MODEL RAILWAY
by Michael Andress
Model railway expert Michael Andress shares the secrets of achieving a wide range of realistic effects, described and illustrated with amazing photographs which will make you look at least twice and ask 'Is it a model – or is it real...?'

PSL BOOK OF MODEL RAILWAY TRACK PLANS
by Cyril Freezer
Whether you are lucky enough to have a free room specially for your layout or are restricted to a corner of the living-room, one of these seventy track plans will meet your requirements.

RAILWAY MODELLING
6th edition
by Norman Simmons
With over 75,000 copies sold, this latest edition of Britain's best-selling model railway book has been completely revised, reset and substantially re-illustrated.
'...the bible of railway modelling...' *Railnews*.